TO *sing*
ALONG
THE WAY

TO sing ALONG THE WAY

Minnesota Women Poets from Pre-Territorial Days to the Present

Edited by
Joyce Sutphen,
Thom Tammaro
& Connie Wanek

© 2006 Edited by Joyce Sutphen, Thom Tammaro, Connie Wanek
First Edition. Third Printing.
Library of Congress Control Number: 2005932916
ISBN-13: 978-0-89823-232-5
ISBN-10: 0-89823-232-5
A Many Minnesotas Series Book
Cover design and interior book design by Christopher Larson and SueAnn Lutkat
Front cover painting, *Sails on Lake Minnetonka*, by Ada A. Wolfe. Used with permission of
Minnesota Historical Society.

The publication of *To Sing Along the Way: Minnesota Women Poets from Pre-Territorial Days to the
Present* is made possible by the generous support of the McKnight Foundation and other
contributors to New Rivers Press.

For academic permission please contact Frederick T. Courtright at 570-839-7477 or
permdude@eclipse.net. For all other permissions, contact The Copyright Clearance
Center at 978-750-8400 or info@copyright.com.

New Rivers Press is a nonprofit literary press associated with Minnesota State
University Moorhead.

Wayne Gudmundson, Director
Alan Davis, Senior Editor
Thom Tammaro, Poetry Editor
Donna Carlson, Managing Editor
      Editorial Assistant: Michelle Roers
      Graduate Assistant: Andria Tieman
      To Sing Along the Way editorial assistant: Crystal Gibbins
      Editorial Interns: Jeff Armstrong, Samuel Beaudoin, Greg Boose,
          Rebeca Dassinger, Crystal Gibbins, Joel Hagen,
          Michelle E. Peterson, Stephanie Schilling,
          Heather Steinmann, Jered Weber
      Design Interns: Melissa Davidson, Brooke Kranzler,
          Christopher Larson, SueAnn Lutkat, Dan Swenson,
          Lindsay Vanhoecke
      Festival Coordinator: Heather Steinmann
      Assistant Festival Coordinator: Miranda Quast
      Web Site Intern: Lindsey Young
Deb Hval, Business Manager
Allen Sheets, Design Manager
Liz Conmy, Marketing Manager

Printed in the United States of America.

New Rivers Press
c/o MSUM
1104 7th Avenue South
Moorhead, MN 56563
www.newriverspress.com

To all the singers along the way

"If earth has a Paradise, it is here."

—HARRIET BISHOP
Minnesota Territory promoter
and school teacher, 1847

Introduction

"As a romantic child of fifteen, I promised myself to 'sing along the way.' And I have kept my word after a fashion."

—ELAINE GOODALE EASTMAN

In many ways, the life of Elaine Goodale Eastman (1863-1953) illustrates the complex challenges women have faced during the past century-and-a-half, if they wanted to be poets, serious poets, in Minnesota or anywhere. Her lines above, from which we take the title of this anthology, were written when she was in her sixties. With her sister Dora, she had published three books of poems by the time she was sixteen years old (1879), and had seen them acclaimed in *The Nation* and *The Atlantic Monthly*. One reviewer, so impressed with the girls' virtuosity at so young an age, remarked, "Really there has never before been a time in literature when a young thrush and a bobolink have printed a book!"

And yet her biographical essay, "All the Days of My Life," which was included in her last collection of poetry, *The Voice at Eve* (1930)—her only collection as a mature adult—was tinged with regret. "Whether we make events, or they make us, is a question which will probably never be satisfactorily answered," she begins her summing up. What had she to regret?

At the age of twenty she had traveled from her childhood home in Massachusetts to the Hampton Institute in Virginia to train as a teacher of Native Americans. She had gone next to Dakota, then a territory, and opened a "day school" near a Sioux village. She learned Sioux and after several years was named by President Harrison as the first supervisor of all Sioux schools, favoring day schools over boarding schools, which she considered cruel. She even traveled over a summer with the Sioux to hunt antelope in the desert Southwest, writing all the while for eastern newspapers and taking up the Sioux cause at every turn.

The massacre at Wounded Knee found her a dozen miles away, close enough to hear the guns. Wounded women and children were transported from the battlefield to a makeshift hospital in a church, where Elaine Goodale helped care for them. She fell in love there, in that tragic place and time, with a young Sioux doctor, Charles Eastman, and they married soon afterwards.

"How simple it all seemed to me then...," she wrote. "From blazing a new path I returned to the old and well-worn road, trodden by women's feet throughout the ages." She raised six children, two of whom were born in St. Paul. She wrote "pot boilers" (as she called them)—novels, four books for young readers, plays, and pageants. She served as her husband's amanuensis and booking secretary as he became famous as a lecturer. She started a summer camp and ran it for ten years in an effort to stabilize the family's finances.

Remarkable vigor, courage, accomplishments, self-sacrifice. And yet she meant to be a poet. As she collected, for *The Voice at Eve*, "scattered verses" that had "appeared in the magazines over a stretch of more than half a century," she wrote, "How broken-winged they flutter and fall, beside the soaring dreams of youth!" What is a poem, that she should so value it so highly in relation to all she had accomplished?

She answers: "I hold that a poem is no trifle of ornament, but a structural reality. It is a drop of the concentrated essence of living. A conception that is held with a certain degree and quality of emotional intensity takes form, as it were, spontaneously—crystallizes in verse as naturally as a snow-flake explodes in a miniature marvel of stars within stars."

We present this anthology not as a record of what women might have written if they'd only been given a chance, but rather as what they have in fact accomplished, and continue to accomplish, in their passion for words and the power of the poem to give enduring meaning to their thoughts, beliefs, and daily lives.

Our anthology begins with the earliest poetic work on Minnesota soil, the oral song-poems of Ojibwe women. Although they are somewhat controversial, we offer translations by the well-known "song catcher" Frances Densmore, for their historical significance, because she herself wrote poetry, and finally because she was from Red Wing.

When we began researching early Minnesota women poets, we had no idea what to expect. How many were there? Who were they? What did they write about? It's not surprising that we had to learn, ourselves, to "read" formal poetry all over again. Margarette Ball Dickson, named Poet Laureate of Minnesota by the Poet Laureate League, Washington, D.C., in 1934, wrote many books, but significantly, two of them were called *Patterns for Poems* and *More Patterns for Poems*. These were collections of poetry that illustrated particular forms—forms within forms, forms upon forms! At that time *verse libre* was grudgingly acknowledged to require some skill, but certainly not as much virtuosity as formal poetry. Even Robert Frost famously compared free verse to playing tennis without a net. Margaret Ball Dickson founded the Dickson-Haining School of Creative Writing in Staples, Minnesota, in 1931, and one feels fairly safe in saying that blocks away people might have heard them rhyming all afternoon.

The foreword to a book by Nan Fitz-Patrick called *Winding Road*, published in 1945, is instructive. It was written by a "distinguished poet, writer, and lecturer" named Clement Wood. He compares Fitz-Patrick to "the latest worthless Pulitzer Poetry Prize winner" T.S. Eliot and finds the former to be an "outstanding and inspiring American poet" while the latter is contemptible, one of the "vacuums who strut as America's Modern Bards." He singles out these lines by Fitz-Patrick as far superior to any worthless "Eliotics":

> And April calls across the mist
> That veils the lake with amethyst.

We know today how this argument ended, for a time, but is such an argument ever really over?

Tastes change, and among our contemporary contributors are relatively few who would attempt to channel their thoughts into strict iambics wherein shine June moons. Perhaps in a hundred years people will read the poetry we are writing today and consider it to be hopelessly old-fashioned. Sometimes during our research we scanned verse in yellowed, delicate pages that seemed embarrassingly bad, and we smiled. Other times the words just caught fire, so current did they seem. Poems like Louise Leighton's "To American Mothers," written just after World War II, are intensely contemporary.

We would like to commend the single book that we relied upon most in our search for early Minnesotan women poets, which was an anthology first published in 1934 and republished in an expanded version in 1938, *Minnesota Verse*, edited by Maude Schilplin. This book included both men and women, of course, but it was so very thorough in scope that we found few poets of that era who were not part of Schilplin's table of contents. It led us to nearly everyone who had published a book, which was one of our criteria in deciding whether there might be work enough to pursue by a particular poet. And the Schilplin anthology confirmed something very important: women wrote a great deal of poetry in the "old days." Many of our grandmothers loved poetry, memorized and quoted poetry, we remember. And wrote it, too. Poetry was frequently published in newspapers and magazines like *Harper's* and *Good Housekeeping* and was part of ordinary discourse. It was said that at one time every home in Texas had a volume of the poems of Grace Noll Crowell, a Minnesotan who relocated to Texas, wrote for money, and sold millions of books. Hers are skilled pieces, but most contemporary women would throw her books across the room because of their sentimental promotion of traditional women's roles.

And women are prolific writers today as well. We were gratified by the number of poets who submitted work for our consideration, as well as the quality of their work, and had there not been space limitations, we could have presented many more moving, wise, invigorating, sassy, funny poems within these covers. One of our regrets as editors is that we could not have printed a larger sample of work from each poet, and our hope is that readers will seek out the writers they like and read more.

Some of the women in this volume are just starting out as writers and have great futures. When we were looking at the Schilplin anthology, we were struck by the biographical note about Meridel LeSueur: in 1938 she was a promising young writer still living with her mother and father in a house on Harriet Avenue in Minneapolis. And then...

Interesting, too, is the fact that the state of Minnesota has been so enriched by waves of immigration over the decades, and again in recent times, and that is reflected in our body of literature. In fact, the mobility of populations in general proved a challenge to us as editors: who exactly is a Minnesotan? Few women were born, lived all their lives, and died in Hibbing or Cloquet or Bemidji. We pored over guidelines others had used, thought hard, and made decisions that could be challenged but seemed right to us. One example: we decided to include the poet Hazel Hall, even though Oregon duly cherishes her as theirs. She was born in Minnesota, and she should be read and reread. Therefore you will find her work here.

We have heard arguments that we are no longer living in a time when, to paraphrase Virginia Woolf, women require an independent fortune and an anthology of their own. Elizabeth Bishop, many years ago, refused to have her work included in "women only" anthologies and made the point that she wanted no qualifier on the term "poet." That position is not unusual today. Yet we felt that it was important to attempt an exploration of the history of women's poetry in Minnesota, and the smallest expedition into library stacks confirmed our conviction that much was there, and most had been forgotten, and this was unfortunate. We hope this book stands as testimony to the fact that women have written seriously and skillfully on the native soil of our state for centuries.

A last point. Many are the thrills of research. This may sound odd. But to visit the wonderful Minnesota Historical Society library, and request and have brought out to you the fragile treasures of old books, and to read pages that have not seen light for some time, and to find there stirring lines and images, the fruit of an individual consciousness long gone but still here, alive in words, is a profound satisfaction. We learned, to take but one example, that the famed children's writer, Carol Ryrie Brink, author of the Caddie Woodlawn books, was also an accomplished poet who published in *Poetry* and many other places. We include her poem "Bones of the Martyrs," which was awarded "Best Lyric" in *The Gypsy* magazine in 1934 (the judge was Robert Frost). Then, too, what a joy it was to have poems flooding in from every corner of Minnesota as we spread the word about this enterprise to our fellow poets.

There is a story for every woman in this book. We know that women struggled for recognition and serious artistic consideration in the past, and we trust and hope that those times are over. Elaine Goodale Eastman, like most women, was pulled in many directions by motherhood, tradition, financial necessity, love, duty, and the demands of her imagination. And she did, also, with spirit, sing along the way.

During the past two-and-one-half years, as we have criss-crossed the state to meet with each other, researching and shaping the anthology, we have had the good fortune to meet and work with many fine people. To them, we offer our heart-felt thanks and gratitude. Without their assistance, we would still be hip-deep in manuscripts, paper clips and library books. We would like to thank Ginger Jentzen for her valuable editorial and research assistance; Ann Jenkins, Julie Kapke, Vivian Gangl, and Mike Grossman, librarians at the Duluth Public Library; the staff at the Minnesota Historical Society library for helping us locate rare and hard-to-find books and journals; Shirley Johnson, President of the Houston County Historical Society; at the University of Minnesota, Barbara Bezat and Alan Lathrop, who responded to our many queries. Thanks also to Mark Peihl, archivist, Clay County Historical Society, Moorhead, Minnesota. At Minnesota State University Moorhead, we want to thank our colleagues in the library, Stacey Voeller and Diane Schmidt, who assisted us in locating hard-to-find materials, always in a timely fashion. Thanks also to librarians Anna Hulseberg and Barbara Fister at Gustavus Adolphus College and to the college for support of the project. We are grateful to the Arrowhead Regional Arts Council for travel support. We also would like to thank Dr. Lauren Leighton, David R. Brink and Nora Brink Hunter, and the Bridgman family. We are especially grateful to Philip Dentinger, who was on board the project from the very start and who deserves special thanks and recognition—we feel his shaping influence and spirit throughout the collection.

At New Rivers Press, we want to thank Donna Carlson, Alan Davis, Alan Sheets, and Wayne Gudmundson for their receptiveness to our original proposal and for their encouragement and support throughout the project. Because New Rivers Press is a teaching press and is integrated into the curriculum at Minnesota State University Moorhead, students—many of whom go on to earn a Certificate in Publishing offered by the university—work with professional faculty and staff on all aspects of book publishing. Each book published by New Rivers Press is assigned a "book team," responsible for designing, editing, marketing and promoting a book. We want to recognize the book team that worked with us on *To Sing Along the Way*: Suzzanne Kelley and Alyssa Schafer, who developed extensive marketing and promotion plans; Christopher Larson and SueAnn Lutkat, who designed the book. We are especially grateful to Crystal Gibbins, former New Rivers Press intern and MFA student at MSUM, who worked as our editorial assistant—Crystal was timely and attentive to detail in her work for us. We are also grateful to MSUM's Office of Academic Affairs for its support.

Finally, we want to thank the many poets, publishers, and literary estates who have given us permission to reprint poems. We are especially grateful to the contemporary poets for their cooperation, support and enthusiasm for the project. We have made reasonable attempts to locate copyright holders and obtain permission to reprint the poems herein. As editors, we take full responsibility for any errors or oversights in the collection. We will make every effort to correct them—or address any oversights brought to our attention—should the anthology go to a second printing.

JOYCE SUTPHEN, Chaska, Minnesota
THOM TAMMARO, Moorhead, Minnesota
CONNIE WANEK, Duluth, Minnesota

Contents

| | *Anonymous* | Ojibwe Love-charm Songs 27 |

1817–1883 *Harriet Bishop*   from *Minnesota: Then and Now* 28

1818–1887 *Mary Henderson Eastman*   The Wood Spirits and the Maiden 30
                                                               from *Jenny Wade of Gettysburg* 31

1854–1938 *Ida Sexton Searls*   from *Ta-Gosh: An Indian Idyl* 32

1862–1927 *Lily Long*   Black Crows 34
                                                       In Time 34
                                                       The Passing of the Indian,
                                                            from *Radisson, The Voyager; A Verse in Four Acts* 35

1863–1953 *Elaine Goodale Eastman*   Christmas Carol 36
                                                           Harebell 37
                                                           The Cross and the Pagan 38

1865–1948 *Marianne Clarke*   Connecting Stars 39

1867–1957 *Frances Densmore*   The Path of the Moon on Mille Lac 40

1870–1943 *Lily Lawrence Bow*   Blossom Time 41

1872–1942 *Marion Craig Wentworth*   Farewell to Autumn 42

1873–1950 *Edith Thompson*   Dandelions 43
                                                      Kitchen Tea 44
                                                      Mande (Myself) 44

1874–1952 *Mary Cummings Eudy*   A Lovely Loneliness 45
                                                          Love 45
                                                          The Nude 45

1876–1956 *Grace Fallow Norton*   Irina 46
                                                        Make No Vows 47
                                                        from The Miller's Youngest Daughter 48

1877-1968	*Nellie Manley Buck*	Bobbed Hair 50
1877-1969	*Grace Noll Crowell*	The Girl That I Used to Be 52
		White Fire 53
1877-1929	*Amy Robbins Ware*	Strike Tents 54
		En Route Again 55
1879-?	*Grace French Smith*	Crosses 56
		Imprisoned Womanhood 57
1880-1964	*Anna Augusta Von Helmholtz-Phelan*	I Lie Quite Still 58
		O Bright, Bright King Tomorrow 58
		The Price 59
1880-1956	*Clara A. Clausen*	Silver Land 60
		The Trees 60
		The Weaver 60
1883-1975	*Nan Fitz-Patrick*	A Letter on Fame to Tu Fu 61
		Summer Night Landscape for Wang Wei 61
1883/4-?	*Maurine Hathaway*	The Captive 62
		The Difference 63
1884-1963	*Margarette Ball Dickson*	Easter 64
		Tumbleweeds 64
1886-1924	*Hazel Hall*	Lingerie 65
		Seams 66
1889-1972	*Hazel Barrington Selby*	Autumn 67
		Wisdom 68
1889-1980	*Gail White*	The Elder Sister 69
1891-1974	*Louise Leighton*	To American Mothers 72
		from Wilderness Journeys, 1659-1661 73
		The Mediterranean 74
1895-1981	*Carol Ryrie Brink*	Bones of the Martyrs 75
		New York Hotel 76
		The Nun 76

1899-1949	Alison Brown	On St. Louis Bay 77
1899-1987	Sister Maris Stella	Grapes 78
		I Who Had Been Afraid 78
		Riddles 79
1900-1996	Meridel LeSueur	Rites of Ancient Ripening 80
1900-1963	Martha Ostenso	She Who Brings Winter 83
		The Farmer's Wife 84
		The Fisherman 85
1900-1989	Carleton Winston	Seven Years Ago 86
1907-1980	Edris Mary Probstfield	A Penny for Your Thoughts 88
		L'envoi 88
1907-1976	Marion Thompson van Steenwyk	Autumn 89
		Quietness 89
1908-1981	Irene Paull	To Bill Heikkila, American 90
		Wall Street Honors the Unknown Soldier 91
1910-1995	Geraldine Ross	Love Potion 94
		Three A.M. 95
1915-1999	Betty Bridgman	The Tire Swing 96
		Letter of Introduction 97
1916	Lucille Broderson	Letter Never Sent 98
1921	Ruth F. Brin	September 99
1926	Mary A. Pryor	Oranges 100
1927	Joanne Hart	Fish 101
1928	Phebe Hanson	Cinderella 102
		Sacred Heart 103
		Sturdy Arms 104
1934	Carol Connolly	Shallows 105

1935   *Edith Rylander*   Too Good to Waste   107

1938   *Jill Breckenridge*   Jacob, Crossing Over   109
                             Will Sommers, Confederate Soldier   110

1940   *Sharon Chmielarz*   Another Love Letter   112

1941   *Florence Chard Dacey*   The Threshold   113

1941   *Diane Glancy*   American Miniaturist   115

1941   *Eva Hooker*   So Unlike Any Simple Thing I Know   117

1941   *Mary Kay Rummel*   A Little Helper   118

1942   *Margot Fortunato Galt*   Relations   119

1942   *Susan Carol Hauser*   Acorn   120

1942   *Martha George Meek*   Saint Stranger   122

1942   *Monica Ochtrup*   Alone   124

1942   *Nancy Paddock*   Bombers   125

1942   *Madelon Sprengnether*   Lot's Wife   127

1942   *Cary Waterman*   After the Pig Butchering   128
                          Me Learning to Dance   129

1943   *Patricia Barone*   Last Night on a Northern Lake   131

1943   *Nancy Fitzgerald*   Arrival: 1973   133

1944   *Norita Dittberner-Jax*   The Feast of the Holy Family   135

1944   *Julie Landsman*   Laos on the Radio   136

1944   *Roseann Lloyd*   *Natt Og Dag*: Return to Norway
                          After 25 Years   138

1944   *Freya Manfred*   Inside the Boat House   139

1944	Mary Rose O'Reilley	The Foster Child 140
1946	Patricia Hampl	St. Paul: Walking 141
		The Moment 141
		Who We Will Love 142
1947	Linda Back McKay	Watermelon Hill 144
1948	Nancy Frederiksen	Flying Blue Angel 146
1948	Jean Jacobson	Skater 147
1949	Patricia Kirkpatrick	A Road in Northern Minnesota 148
1949	Joyce Sutphen	What to Pack 149
1950	Vicki Graham	Solstice 150
1950	Margaret Hasse	In a Sheep's Eye, Darling 151
1950	Deborah Keenan	Loving Motels 153
1951	Ethna McKiernan	The Scholar in the Playroom 155
1951	CarolAnn Russell	Fishing 156
1951	Ann Taylor Sargent	21 Postcards 157
1952	Marisha Chamberlain	Winter Washday 159
1952	Mary Logue	Song in Killeshandra 160
1952	Francine Sterle	Flat-backed Fox 161
1952	Connie Wanek	Jump Rope 162
1954	Louise Erdrich	Advice to Myself 163
		Owls 164
		Rez Litany 165
1954	Gail Rixen	Shell River 167
1954	Susan Steger Welsh	In Defense of Semicolons 168

1955   *Sandy Beach*   Slow Brown Fox   169

1955   *Candace Black*   Vigil   170

1956   *Kate Lynn Hibbard*   Kleptomania   171

1956   *Leslie Adrienne Miller*   Up North   172
                                    Bridal Wear   173

1956   *Sheila Packa*   The Vermilion Trail   175

1957   *Wang Ping*   Opening the Face   177
                       What Holds   179

1957   *Jane Whitledge*   What It Was Like   180

1958   *Ellie Schoenfeld*   If I Were the Moon   182

1959   *Diane Jarvenpa*   Night Walk to the Sauna   183

1959   *Athena Kildegaard*   After the Death of His Brother's Wife   184

1960   *Kathryn Kysar*   The Pregnant Wife Eats Dirt   185

1960   *Elizabeth Oness*   Belleek   186

1962   *Kirsten Dierking*   Northern Oracle   188

1963   *Betsy Brown*   Hallways of a Diamond: January 2004   189

1963   *Heid Erdrich*   Animoosh   191
                         Stung   192

1963   *Juliet Patterson*   Index of First Lines   193

1964   *Cullen Bailey Burns*   I Have Made a Paper Boat   194

1964   *Kelly Everding*   Omens   195

1965   *Deidre Pope*   Anticipating Hoarfrost   196

1969   *Pacyinz Lyfoung*   She No Zen   197

1969   *Anna George Meek*   Democratic Vistas   198

1970   *April Lott*   Kitchen Sketch with Government
                           Surplus   199

1971   *Katrina Vandenberg*   Record   200

1974   *Sun Yung Shin*   The Tourist's Prayer Bead Bracelet   202

1979   *May M. Lee*   Keys   204

For Further Reading   206

Contributors   209

About the Artist   234

About the Editors   235

Permissions   236

TO sing ALONG THE WAY

Ojibwe Love-charm Songs
Collected by Frances Densmore (1867-1957)

No.71

A´ ninajun´
Ogĭni´ baguň´
Ajina´gooyan´

What are you saying to me?
I am arrayed like the roses
And beautiful as they

No.72

Niwawin´gawia´
Ĕnĭ´nīwa´

I can charm the man
He is completely fascinated
by me

No.73

Ninda´agagia´
I´enĭ´ni
Namundj´
Ĕn´dogwĕn´
Wi´agudjiûg´

I can make that man bashful. I
wonder what can be the matter
that he is so bashful

Harriet Bishop (1817–1883)

from *Minnesota: Then and Now*

March, eighteen hundred forty-nine,
    A daughter hale and pretty
Was born to honorable Uncle Sam,
    Who named her Minnesota.

From running in the open air,
    In limpid streamlets bathing,
Her cheeks grew very fat and fair,
    With golden tresses waving.

Her brain was clear, her footsteps free,
    Her pleasant ways were winning,
And she was always in the right,
    Unless when she was sinning.

So Uncle Samuel petted her,
    As children few are petted,
And it has been her filial care
    That it be not regretted.

Ripening in youthful beauty,
    As he had never seen,
He put her in long dresses
    Before she reached her teens.

Now lend an ear and you shall hear,
    How well she has repaid him
For his fond love paternal,
    For all the trouble made him;

She's never flinched when duty called,
    She's never shrinked from working,
And never, in dark peril's hour,
    Has sought a place for lurking.

Her own right arm has wonders wrought,
    In building towns and cities,
In roads and bridges, farms and homes,
    And sings them in her ditties.

Old Plymouth rock has echoed back
    The invitation given—
Its precious seed of Truth and Right,
    Have been her moral leaven.

Her voice is heard across the wave,
    Off'ring to other nations
The blessings of the "Homestead Act,"
    With clothes and daily rations.

And well have been repaid her smiles
    On foreign sons and daughters,
Who boast to-day their first owned homes
    In land of Laughing Waters.

MARY EASTMAN (1818-1887)

The Wood Spirits and the Maiden

THOSE WHO HAVE LIVED AMONG THE INDIANS ARE ACCUSTOMED TO
THEIR FAITH IN THE PROTECTING POWER OF THE SPIRITS OF
NATURE. ESPECIALLY POWERFUL IS THE GOD OF THE WOODS AND
FORESTS.

Day with its gorgeous light passes away,
Shadows of coming night darken the way.
> Who is the wanderer
> With the long braided hair?
> 'Mid the tall evergreens,
> She like a fairy seems;
> Know ye the maiden young,
> Wood Spirits, say?

Know we the maiden young—mark well her form,
Like the tall pine tree, when rages the storm.
> How like the dark bird's wing
> Glistens her braided hair.
> When watching o'er her birth,
> Sang we a song of earth,
> We were her guardians made,
> She was our child.

Soon o'er her body cold, chaunt we her funeral hymn,
Wild branches, torn and old, timing the requiem.
> Why does she wander here,
> With the long braided hair?
> Why is the maiden pale—
> Why does her breathing fail?
> Now, by the moonbeams fair,
> See her dimmed eye.

She loved as maiden loves, she wept as woman weeps.
Soon will her restless frame sleep where her lover sleeps.

> Then to our far-off groves
> Will we her spirit bear.
> When heaves her parting sigh,
> When closed her lustrous eye,
> We will her guardians be,—
> She is our child.

from *Jenny Wade of Gettysburg*

Pale as a lily Jenny's face,
And in her temples you could trace
The blue veins, over which her hair
Shone like the waves of Delaware,
When the sun's burning glances stream
Their lustre where the billows dream;
Her hands and arms were white as snow;
Well used to labor were they, though,
For idleness and Jenny Wade
Had never yet acquaintance made;
Her waist was trim and small and round,
And ever with an apron bound,
White as the flour she sifted o'er
The loaves ranged by the oven-door.

Ida Sexton Searles (1854–1938)

from *Ta-Gosh: An Indian Idyl*

Prologue

I

Tall and sombre rise the pine trees
    On the cliffs of Fond-du-Lac;
Still they sigh and whisper sadly
    Of the days that come not back;
Days when deer and moose abounded;
    Trout went gliding through the streams;
Here, in Northern Minnesota
    Where the red-eyed furnace gleams,

Stood the forest, vast, primeval,
    Speaking of long ages past,
While beneath it vaster riches
    Nature's lavish hand had cast:
Coal and iron and copper hidden
    'Neath the timbered wealth above,
Where the red-man built his wigwam,
    Hunted game, or wooed his love.

Simple were these nomad people
    Who, one hundred years ago,
Lived and loved and toiled and suffered—
    Ah, how little do we know
Of their history or traditions!
    Wild and barbarous they were,
Yet their noble deeds of daring
    Often might our pulses stir.

II

All about us, superstitions
    Haunt the spots they held in dread:
There, on lonely Spirit Island
    Shades of warriors long since dead
Lead the Ghost Dance, so they tell us.
    Now, if you would listen more,
Hear these Indian traditions,
    Echoes, faint, of vanished lore:

Where the white-man's buildings crumble—
    Ask the red-man—he will say:
"They were built within the ghost line,
    Where they doom all to decay."
Bald and barren, see "Wad-ji-win",
    Where they fasted ten long days;
Now upon its rocky summit,
    No lone youth for guidance prays.

III

Priceless boon, one great survival
    Has been theirs for times untold;
When the Spaniard crossed the ocean,
    It was then a custom old;
Coming thus down through the ages,
    All their joys have been enhanced,
All their sorrows been forgotten,
    In the stately tribal dance.

Young and old join in the measure,
    Circling 'round the sacred drum;
To invoke Manitou's blessing,
    All the tribes, in reverence, come.

Lily Long (1862-1927)

Black Crows

Crows upon a corn-field, fighting for their own,
Taking in a harvest where they have not sown,
Knowing well their hunger,—knowing that alone.

Life at its beginning nothing but a maw!—
Fierce in its insistence on the primal law.
Crows upon a corn-field!—More than crows I saw.

In Time

The tide is coming in.
    Its soft, wet fingers smooth and wipe away
    The mounds of sand where idle dreamers lay,
    And mimic forts that children reared in play,
And fought to win.

I saw a tower today
    Built by a king of olden time to tame
    Wild people, and ensure his deathless fame.
    The tower an ivied ruin; and his name—
I do not know.

The Passing of the Indian
from RADISSON, THE VOYAGER; A VERSE DRAMA IN FOUR ACTS

A mist that shifts and changes with the wind,
A dream the dreamer tries in vain to hold,—
Such is the mastery on the earth of man.
Where once the unfettered Redman roamed at will,
The white man claims the land by metes and bounds.
The clang of mill and factory breaks the hush
That brooded on the prairie and the stream,
And where the moccasin flower, shy and wild,
Danced with the wind and sheltered in the shade,
The prim, trim fields march straitly, row by row.
What has been, shall be; change shall follow change.
For the dominion that man claims is vain,
His lordship of the earth a passing dream,—
A dream the dreamer tries in vain to clasp,
A mist that melts within his futile grasp.

Elaine Goodale Eastman (1863–1953)

Christmas Carol

Our walls are wreathed with trailing pine,
    And hemlock boughs are leaning
Dark where the blood-red berries shine,
    With leaves of Autumn's gleaning;
Yet ah! how pale the Summer's pride,
    How barren field and fallow,—
For why? the year must be so wide,
    And Summer still so narrow!

Our chimneys glow with generous heat,
    And all our lamps are burning,
We list the music wild and sweet,
    With dance and song returning;
Yet oh! the vaster dark outside,
    How cold and dumb with sorrow!
For still the world must be so wide,
    And joy, alas! so narrow!

Our home throws wide its doors to-night,
    Our threshold laughs with greeting;
With clasp as warm and step as light
    The old-time friends are meeting;
Yet oh! the few who stand aside
    Bowed down by hopeless sorrow,
And weep that hearts should be so wide,
    And love, alas! so narrow!

Nay, further press the strong desire,
    The questioning, swift yet tender,
And lifted ever strangely higher,
    Divine a holier splendor;
On Christmas-day, whate'er betide,
    We have no room for sorrow,
For though man's need be e'er so wide,
    God's help grows never narrow.

Harebell

Low adown the gracious meadow, dappled close
    with sun and shadow,
Rounded soft by waving grasses, thro' a hundred
    falling lines,
Drowsy as the noontide found her, with her ample
    robes around her,
Summer, lost in idle musing, at her ease reclines.

Floating free in dell and hollow, ere the fleetfoot
    daisies follow,
Springing light where swoon the breezes, warm
    against her throbbing breast,
Pure and deep, yet swaying lowly to a rhythm sweet
    and holy,
Myriad harebells meet and tremble o'er her dream-
    less rest.

High above the quiet valley, where she loves to
    droop and dally,
All along the windy headlands, where the rock is
    steep and bare,
Summer stays a moment only,—leaves her kingdom
    wild and lonely,
And her warm breath chills to vapor on the frosty
    air.

Yet in bleak and barren places, fresh with unex-
    pected graces,
Leaning over rocky ledges, tenderest glances to
    bestow,
Dauntless still in time of danger, thrilling every
    wayworn stranger,
Scattered harebells earn a triumph never known
    below!

The Cross and the Pagan

As men in the forest, erect and free,
We prayed to God in the living tree;
You razed our shrine, to the wood-god's loss,
And out of the tree you fashioned a Cross!

You left us for worship one day in seven;
In exchange for our earth you offered us heaven;
Dizzy with wonder, and wild with loss,
We bent the knee to your awful Cross.

Your sad, sweet Christ—we called him Lord;
He promised us peace, but he brought a sword;
In shame and sorrow, in pain and loss,
We have drunk his cup; we have borne his Cross!

MARIANNE CLARKE (1865-1948)

Connecting Stars

Twilight has gaged a connection
With the magical realm above,
Stella related to Castor
And to Pollux, the two I love.

It is indeed inspiring
To rise in the air, at times,
From the earth somewhat too worldly,
In its human pantomimes.

Sparkles appeared in the darkness,
Leda dwelt with the King of Spain,
Mother of mythical children
In the Greek astronomical reign.

Pollux is known as immortal,
Castor shares with his twin,
Jewels gleam in the distance,
With brilliance of kith and kin.

Birthdays arranged for bright Stella
Are the link of celestial wings,
June, as the thrilling infusion,
Pentecostal in powerful things.

Gemini pleased our own Stella
With companionship's voice on high,
Kind invitations to visit,
Forever singing: "Here am I."

Frances Densmore (1867–1957)

The Path of the Moon on Mille Lac

Greeting, O sons of the white man,
Who come to the land of our fathers,
Welcome to shores that are lovely,
To pines and to forest abundant.

You will build houses and fences
Where we have lived in a wigwam,
But you cannot find the wood-spirit
Nor talk with the god of the water.

Stories our fathers have told us
Will never be told to your children—
Stories of wolf and of rabbit,
Our brothers who live in the woodland.

Ours is the memory of starlight
On miles of untrodden snow fields,
Silence and rest from intrusion
Were ours, but have vanished forever.

The forest will bow to the axes
And the pines will never come back,
But one thing will stay here forever,
The path of the moon on Mille Lac.

LILY LAWRENCE BOW (1870–1943)

Blossom Time

One day the plum trees bloomed
And draped a curtain,
A pink film over the hillside.
They shed their petals,
And like drifts of tinted snow
Lay upon the ground.

The soft wind gave wings to some,
Wafting them along,
Some fell into the river
And sailed down stream,
Dying the waters pale pink,
Floated out to sea.

Marion Craig Wentworth (1872-1942)

Farewell to Autumn

A day of vermilion and gold,
Veiled in haze and mock summer heat,
Now dreams the hours away,
Secure in glory and full-ripened power;

(Only a crackling shudder
Ripples the scarlet,
Confesses a weakness—)

Dreams through the flare of the sunset,
Bravely on into the dark,
Unaware of the fatal ambush
That lurks in the turn of the night,
Until, all at once, it is grasped
By a wind—a Fury!

The sleeper,
Half-roused by the shriek,
Shivers, draws closer the coverlet,
Sleeps on—
Dull to the pitiless onslaught without,
The swirling, the stripping,
The dumb, helpless surrender of beauty.

But his surprise next morning:
All the glory gone—*in one night!*
While the bare limbs of the maples cry out
In the hurt of too sudden nakedness—
Pleading with the laughter
Of the clear exultant air.

Edith Thompson (1873-1950)

Dandelions

I

The gypsy flowers are come again,
   Millions and millions!
Dandelions twinkle here
   In billions and trillions
On every waste and wayside green.

Gypsies make dandelion wine,
   Cut tender leaves for salads,
Brew coffee from the roasted root
   And find heart-lift for ballads
On every bright-eyed wayside green.

2

Give us only a week or two
   To star your lawn or lane,
And another week for our silvery moons
   To wax and wane,
And you may have the rest of the year
   Without our smiling stare,
For we've blown our glimmering bubbles of seed
   Ev-er-y-where.

"I just hate dandelions,"
   My kindly neighbor said,
But, being fair, she added,
   "I s'pose when I am dead
They will remember where I lie,
   And sprinkle my small plot
With golden glimmer in the spring
   When all others have forgot."

Kitchen Tea

I drink my cup of kitchen tea
And listen to the kettle sing
Its song of water, wind and fire,
And their commingling.

Around the cup that holds the tea,
Blue willow, river, lovers, birds,
A tale of water, wind and human fire,
Told without words.

Mande (Myself)

I stopped to drink of a nameless spring
    Beside an unmarked road,
And there I met an unknown man
    Bent by an unseen load,

Dark and eager and thirsty
    With seeking, lonely eye,
Framed in the grassy, wayside spring
    Against a quiet sky.

MARY CUMMINGS EUDY (1874-1952)

A Lovely Loneliness

There is a lovely loneliness,
A quietness of self
Whereby we find the sky
A cloak upon our back;
We wrap it close about us,
Cover head as with a cowl.
When silence is too broken,
We've scarce a self
To wrap at all.

Love

Some joys are soft as summer rain
And sift their sweetness
Through the silt
Of heavy days.

Other joy strikes hard
Till afterward...we ask
If it were joy...or pain.
And almost pray it may not come again.

The Nude

The form I worship is the nude:
Not human symmetry,
But thought by words uncovered
Till to the mind unveiled
Stands Poetry in perfect form
As thought...freeborn.
The form I worship is the nude.

GRACE FALLOW NORTON (1876–1956)

Irina

Because it is so cold and gray
    I dream wine and the south.
Because I love no man on earth
    I dream of your warm mouth.

How I would touch my glass to yours!
    How golden it would ring!
Because of the bleakness and the gray
    I let it thrill and sting,

The song that from your heart would fly
    When I had touched its core
With warmth of mine and wine of mine—
    O your heart's waiting door!

Because I love you not, nor yet
    Would feel your hand o'er mine,
I dare this play in a drear day,
    With dream-warmth and dream-wine.

Make No Vows

I made a vow once, one only.
I was young and I was lonely.
When I grew strong I said: "This vow
Is too narrow for me now.
Who am I to be bound by old oaths?
I will change them as I change my clothes!"

But that ancient outworn vow
Was like fetters upon me now.
It was hard to break, hard to break;
Hard to shake from me, hard to shake.

I broke it by day, but it closed upon me at night.
He is not free who is free only in the sunlight.
He is not free who hears fetters in his dreams,
Nor he who laughs only by dark dream-fed streams.

Oh, it costs much bright coin of strength to live!
Watch, then, where all your strength you give!
For I, who would be so wild and wondrous now,
Must give, give, to break a burdening bitter vow.

From *The Miller's Youngest Daughter*

9

In the wood she had her house,
  An acorn for her dipper,
Made her bed of white birch boughs,
  Of sorrel made her supper;

And O she was a shiftless dove,
  Ate her breakfast at night,
Hung her wash up Saturday eve
  To bleach by white moonlight,

Wove her clothes of thistle-shred
  And silky milkweed-tatters—
"For they are very pretty," she said,
  "And nothing really matters

"Till I learn to understand
  Everything that is;
The miller is mighty in the land,
  The high mill is his,

"Makes music for him when he
  Goes out, when he comes in,

And yet all things make music for me,
  Whose going was a sin."

Thus his erring daughter sings
  Of the miller's strength.
The lovely music of all things
  She learns to praise at length.

II

Winter held his cold cup to her mouth.
Like a swallow she flew south
And sang on her way as sweet and loud as she could
The songs that she had learned in the wood
And all the songs that she had thought to sing
About the meaning of everything.

An old man at the gate of a smoking city
Tossed her a penny out of pity;
A woman in a shady village street
Gave her a piece of bread to eat;
A child who fed her on a wide green lawn
Said she had fed a little white fawn;

A boy she met could only pant and cry,
"I've seen the little white moon go by!"

Nellie Manley Buck (1877-1968)

Bobbed Hair

Pa says to ma: "It's a holy fright,
When I go to the barber shop,
And have to wait for some old hen—
Who's tryin' to flap and flop!
A gettin' her hair cut in a bob!
An' me—just standin' around—
Right in a *man's barber shop*—
'Cause she's first on the ground!

If *my* wife cuts off her hair,
(And pa looked so awful mad!)
I'll get a divorce, you bet your life!
That's what I'll do!" says dad.
"Don't see why women cut their hair,—
'Specially with grown-up girls,—
Tryin' to look like one of them,
With a lot of silly curls!"

Ma says to pa: "It's the darn'dest sight,
That everywhere one goes,
One sees that Charlie Chaplin thing
Stuck under some man's nose!—
If I do cut off my hair,
It won't spoil the front of my head!—
And wearing that silly Chaplin thing,—
Say! *I wouldn't be caught dead!*"

Then pa went down and had it cut,—
His little pet mustache!
Afraid that ma would bob her hair!
And then,—but Oh, my gosh!

When pa came home, his face all grins,
At the sacrifice he'd done,
Ma met him right square in the door,—
And you should have seen the fun!
Ma had her hair all cut off short,
Marcelled in the cutest curl!—
And pa,—just put his arms right 'round ma,
An' said, "*Oh, you darling girl!!!*"

Grace Noll Crowell (1877-1969)

The Girl That I Used To Be

She came tonight as I sat alone,
The girl that I used to be,
And she gazed at me with her earnest eyes,
And questioned reproachfully:
"Have you forgotten the many plans,
And hopes that I had for you;
The great career, the splendid fame.
All the wonderful things to do?
Where is the mansion of stately height,
With its grounds and its gardens rare,
The silken robes that I dreamed for you,
And the jewels for your hair?"
And as she spoke I was very sad,
For I wanted her pleased with me—
This slender girl from the shadowy past,
The girl that I used to be.

So, gently arising I took her hand
And guided her up the stair,
Where peacefully sleeping my babies lay,
Innocent, sweet and fair.
And I told her that they are my only gems,
And precious they are to me;
That my silken robe is my motherhood,
Of costly simplicity,
And my mansion of stately height is Love,
And the only career I know
Is serving each day in its sheltering walls
For the dear ones who come and go.
And as I spoke to my shadow guest,
She smiled through her tears at me,
And I saw that the woman that I am now,
Pleased the girl that I used to be.

White Fire

The first star burns like white fire on the hill;
Listen, my heart, did some one call my name?
"Through the blue dusk—a voicing whippoorwill;
In the primrose west, there is only a white star's flame."
How does the aching beauty of this hour
Recall to me an unremembered thing?
O heart, why do you turn like a swaying flower?
I wonder, little wild night bird, how you can sing?

A pale moth beats its wings at a lattice bar;
The petals of a moon-flower have unfurled,
Close to the waiting star—a radiant star—
Has leaped to his love across a chasmed world.
(O heart, be like a star steadfast and bright—
Two fires are burning on the hill tonight.)

Amy Robbins Ware (1877–1929)

Strike Tents

Field Hospital #41, September 18th, 1918

Last night a fragment of shrapnel shell
    Dropped by a bird of the night,
Struck one of the men from my home town
    As it swerved in its death-dealing flight.

He died in the span of a moment
    With his poor throat mangled and torn.
It was only a few yards from where I sat;
    And they laid him to rest in the early morn.

So the C.O. ordered a zigzag trench
    Dug through the stony soil,
To make us safe from the "daisy cutters"
    By this urgently strenuous toil.

Just as our dearly wrought promenade
    Was ready against the need,
Came commands "Break camp immediately,
    And on sealed orders proceed."

We have pulled up stakes and packed our stores,
    And now we are on the way
To another spot in the U.S. line
    For another fight on another day.

En Route Again

Vaubricourt to Brizeaux-Forestière,
Meuse-Argonne, September 26th, 1918.

This noon Capt. Pennington asked me if I could be
ready to move on in 45 minutes, so we're off!

Another hospital with no Red Cross at all
Is in most tragic need of help that we could give,
So Captain Pennington is sending us still further up.
With such equipment, we can make a shift to live,
The while we set up our establishment out there,
To carry on the work which meets one everywhere.

Lieutenant Hoyle and I were leaving Number Nine
In a camion filled with many strange supplies,—
Cots and lumber, stoves, bricks, mortar, marmites, blankets,
Tar paper, nails, and food for needs that might arise.
As we were starting from the Camp at Vaubricourt,
Came Margaret Brown in search of missing Mobile 4.

So we joined forces, and away we drove together,
Tossing cigarettes and bars of chocolate as we went,
To marching men, en route to the inferno just ahead,
From which yet others are returning weary, spent.
Of these who march beside us on the muddy way,
How many will be carried back to us today!

GRACE FRENCH SMITH (1879-?)

Crosses

White crosses—black crosses—
On the hills of France!
Beneath them lies an army of the dead.
Stirred by propaganda men came, men died,
Cannon fodder in France.

White crosses—black crosses—
Let the dead rise from their graves and march,

Twenty abreast—twenty abreast—
The silent tread of destroyed men!
Eleven days for the British to pass—
Ten days for the French—
Three weeks of Russia's dogged step—
Four weeks for the Central Powers—
America follows,
And men from far corners of the Earth.

Genius slain—art and statesmanship;
Wisdom gone—invention and research;
Love gone and the deep things of God.

Tramp, tramp—eternal tramp!
This silent tread of destroyed men.
At the end, out of the mist, comes Christ dragging a cross,
His form is bent and the cross drips blood,
We have crucified the Lord of Love afresh—
The Prince of Peace.

Imprisoned Womanhood

Through the lattice bars of a harem's pall,
As she obeys her lord's commands—
Tear drops, fall.

Through the iron bars of custom's wall,
Abused and crushed in many lands—
Tear drops, fall.

Through the ages she has swallowed gall,
And stumbled over drifting sands.
Trumpet, call!

At last she is finding justice's hall,
And slowly breaking iron bands—
Trumpet call!

Anna Augusta Von Helmholtz-Phelan
(1880-1964)

I Lie Quite Still

I lie quite still through the long autumn night
Hearing the wind sing the dirge of the leaves,
Falling so wearily, softly to earth...
And I think of how all things fall ever to Silence,
Ever to stillness, save only the wind...

I lie quite still through the long, autumn night.

O Bright, Bright King Tomorrow

O bright, bright King Tomorrow,
A magic key you wield
That opens every secret door
We thought Today had sealed.

The failures of our present,
The omissions of our past,
We yield to you, bright sovereign.
Our lot with you we cast.

The vast undone, the sinful done,
And all our heavy sorrow,
Too weak to bear alone, we throw
On you, bright King Tomorrow—
O, bright, bright King Tomorrow!

The Price

In ravaged fields Death's prey they lie,
Toll of freedom—blood-bought freedom.
Freedom for a threatened world.
With their young and lissome bodies,
With their forward-looking eyes,
With their dreams and home-sweet visions,
Millions marched and fell and died
To buy freedom for the world!
They thought to buy us safe Tomorrows
With their glorious young Todays!

Though we sent them on fools' errands,
Let us never forget, O Peoples,
For our Tomorrows, their Todays!

CLARA A. CLAUSEN (1880–1956)

Silver Land

Silver moon,
You sail too soon,
O stately ship of might.

Shining star,
It seems you are
A tip of candle-light.

Silver land,
An unknown hand
Guards destinies of night.

The Trees

It almost seems that they can talk,
those trees that stand along the walk.
They look like Grandmas standing there,
With old bent backs and waving hair.
When strong winds come and blow and blow,
I'm sure that they would like to go
Far, far away where they could hide.
Dear me, they can't! Their feet are tied.

The Weaver

Time is a subtle weaver, who scorns the use of gold,
As he patterns threads of silver for those who must grow old.

Nan Fitz-Patrick (1883-1975)

A Letter On Fame to Tu Fu

A pale mist hangs on the mountains at sunrise,
The fragrance of plum petals rides on the wind,
The path of the dawn is gold on the river;
But fame has a substance more fragile and thinned.

Sorrow returns, though we drown it in rivers;
And pain is a fetter of brass on the hand;
But you, who have written the beauty of ages,
Are powdered white bone and pale yellow sand.

A blue candle-lantern is hung in the rain,
And creaks at the gate on a rusty chain.

Summer Night Landscape for Wang Wei

The low moon hangs on a purple treetop,
Orange and wistful above Chung-nan's crest.
The firefly lanterns illume the blue twilight
Beside the clear pool, where the white egrets nest.

Black are the willows against the horizon,
Darker the mind where ambition lurks;
Ashes of gold and gray dust of oblivion
Are all that remain of a man and his works.

And yet, the woodcutter sings at his task;
Yet, sweet is the wine in a moldy cask.

Maurine Hathaway (1883/4-?)

The Captive

Oh, I'm hindered and bound by conventional things,
    And I beat at the bars of my cage
As a wild captive bird beats and bruises its wings
    In the wrath of its weak, helpless rage.

I long to go on as I will in the world,
    Untrammelled and reinless and free,
While these sickening social conventions are hurled
    To the winds of the billowy sea.

I want to be *free* to grasp pleasures I see,
    Which a God-given nature impels,
And to scorn what society thrusts upon me,
    'Gainst which soul, brain and body rebels.

Like a young panther caught while asleep in her lair,
    They have bound and are holding me fast,
While with mad yearning eyes I gaze out at the fair
    Lovely world where I dwelt in the past.

My soul was not meant to be captive, I know,
    And 'twill never be reconciled,
So I tear at the bonds that are holding me so,
    For I long to go back to the wild.

The Difference

Two women loved him. One was cold and pure
As any barren, desolated moor.
The other was a creature, dazzling, bright,
Whose sensuous beauty thrilled him with delight.

He died,—and ere a year had passed away,
The chaste, pure woman wed one summer day;
But when the autumn winds sighed overhead,
The other one who loved him so, was dead.

Margarette Ball Dickson (1884–1963)

Easter

(Memorial)

Pile blossoms for the unnamed ones
Beneath the Spanish field,
And for the host that lie unmarked,
A Siegfried Line revealed;
The bombed and raided innocents
Along the Scottish downs...
The frozen ones who died so far
From little Russian towns;
The splendid skiers of the north,
The lost on Turkish plain
Who can not pluck gold buttercups
Or crocus-bloom again.

Tumbleweeds

I dragged the tumbleweeds from near the fence
And pulled them out of corners here and there.
My hands are full of prickles, I declare,
And now I think of it, the pain's intense.
But while I wrenched them from the currant rows
And pulled them from the clinging dahlia's clasp
I did not seem to sense their sting and rasp,
I was so interested, I suppose.
And now the pile is high, a tangled heap
Each clinging to the other, so it seems,
As aging hearts cling to the early dreams
That, somehow, through the years we always keep;
And we will stand and watch the leaping red,
Forgetting all the toil by which it's fed.

Hazel Hall (1886-1924)

Lingerie

To-day my hands have been flattered
With the cool-finger touch of thin linen,
And I have unwound
Yards of soft, folded nainsook
From a stiff bolt.
Also I have held a piece of lawn
While it marbled with light
In a sudden quiver of sun.

So to-night I know of the delicate pleasure
Of white-handed women
Who like to touch smooth linen handkerchiefs,
And of the baby's tactual surprise
In closing its fist
Over a handful of nainsook,
And even something of the secret pride of the girl
As the folds of her fine lawn nightgown
Breathe against her body.

Seams

I was sewing a seam one day—
Just this way—
Flashing four silver stitches there
With thread, like this, fine as a hair,
And then four here, and there again,
When
The seam I sewed dropped out of sight...
I saw the sea come rustling in,
Big and grey, windy and bright...
Then my thread that was as thin
As hair, tangled up like smoke
And broke.
I threaded up my needle, then—
Four here, four there, and here again.

HAZEL BARRINGTON SELBY (1889-1972)

Autumn

Acquiescent are these trees,
Pale clouds, and winnowed earth...
So has a woman earned her peace
When, travail past,
She knows release,
At last.

Death-wrenched from out a slanted hour
When pain has paid of passion's debt
And seed has curved to fruit and flower,
At worst or best
A woman earns
Her rest.

This grass, these acquiescent trees,
Pale clouds, and weary earth,
Tempered as she in doom of birth
Reap the still breath
And widened mood
Of death.

Wisdom

I have seen the wind uncover
Strange things under snow...
You would be a lusty lover,
That I know:
Better let you go!

Passion is a silly rover
Bogged at last by woe;
Sweet the quest, then it is over,
That I know:
Better let you go!

Sweet-mad, bees will sting in clover
Caring not if friend or foe;
You would be a lusty lover,
That I know:
Better let you go!

GAIL WHITE (1889-1980)

The Elder Sister

In morning sunlight
   On the garden seat
The elder sister works
   For early hours are fleet.

Her active fingers
   Deftly pare and prune
Greens, fresh and crisp,
   For it will soon be noon.

A bowl of eggs
   She whips to golden foam,
An omelet,
   For the children coming home.

Upon the table
   Lays a snowy spread,
Neat cubes of butter,
   Plates of gold-edged bread.

The sudden rush
   Of light impatient feet,
Her mother's children
   Coming home for meat.

Restive as greyhounds,
   They are poised to run,
The elder sister's meal
   Has but begun.

The table cleared,
   The dishes stand in piles,
Some banter of the noon meal
   She recalls, and smiles.

A jug of milk
　　She leaves upon a shelf,
And rusks-
　　Each child may help himself.

An hour of leisure
　　When all-healing sleep would claim,
She'll rouse herself
　　To plan for them again.

　　　　　* * *

She sweeps the floor,
　　And dusts,
From tarnished knives she scours
　　The pirate rust.
Her polished glasses
　　Grace the cupboard shelf;
There is no time
　　To glorify herself.
The window panes
　　Reflect the shining sun,
The elder sister's work
　　Is never done.
Small woolen stockings dangle
　　Two by two,
Matching the other
　　Both in size and hue.
Their texture
　　So consistently demands
The careful work
　　Of patient, loving hands.
And, when the children come
　　At close of day,
How could they find her
　　Young enough to play?

　　　　　* * *

Through years, the twinkling feet
    Grow more sedate,
Then make firm imprints
    Through the garden gate.
And, should adventure claim them
    One by one,
It leaves a trifle less at home
    That must be done.
The elder sister,
    Seeing them depart,
Waves a farewell
    With one hand on her heart.

LOUISE LEIGHTON (1891-1974)

To American Mothers

Now that the war is done,
Let us bury an unknown child
At Arlington.
A child who died alone
On a Chinese street, his body a pitiful
Cage of bone,
Or a child who lived in Greece,
Who cowered in caves and never knew
The ways of peace;
Or take a Jewish child
Whose delicate flesh was burned away
At Buchenwald.
Oh, let us bury here
A child without a name or a nation,
Kneel at the bier,
Never again supine,
But in bitter shame and grief, whispering:
This child was mine.

from "Wilderness Journeys," 1659-1661

I

That year when Pierre and des Grosielliers
Spent the winter in the "Nation of the Oats,"
Many died of hunger.
                    The sun withdrew
Behind the sky and a cloud descended
Upon the earth. Sheathed in brittle ice, the forest
Crackled eerily in a dim twilight. Wet feathers
Of snow wrapped the hunter's ankles,
Tipping him onto his face; mocking his gun
And his hunger; covering berry and root, warning
The bird, and letting the beast escape.
                                    When they
Had eaten all the dogs in the village, they boiled
The bark from vines, or they made a pitiful soup
From old powdered bones dissolved in water; these bitter
Brews made them burn with a frantic thirst.
Last, they scraped the fur from their moccasins
And their beaver robes, gnawing on the rancid skins.
Too weak to build a fire to warm their wigwams,
Many died of freezing. And still the wet snow fell
Day after day from the great pewter dome of the sky.

The Mediterranean

(MAY, 1943)

Across this flowing, fabulous blue,
    A bird soars with unfrightened heart,
While high against a luminous cloud,
    A plane is blown apart.

Now winging fast from shore to shore,
    Fly ibis, pelicans, and doves;
They flew a thousand years ago,
    And still they seek their loves.

The bombs scream down, the hot guns crack;
    Ship after ship bursts into flame;
Vast cargoes spill into the sea,
    And men are but a name.

Yet still the wild birds fly across
    From Libyan sands to Alpine creeks,
Across the ancient olive groves,
    Above the snowy peaks.

The herdsman cowers on the hill,
    A brown child burrows in the moss,
But still among the sounds of doom,
    The wild birds fly across...
    The wild birds fly across.

Carol Ryrie Brink (1895-1981)

Bones of the Martyrs

Baud saw the strangers through the high, grilled gate
And how the little bell wagged up and down
With their impatience,—must not make them wait,
Strangers came seldom now. She smoothed her gown,
Her trembling fingers set her white cap straight,
And, silent as a kitten's feet on down,
She heard her wooden shoes crossing the court.
She saw their mouths open and close with words
But God had sealed her own against retort.
Over their heads she saw a flight of birds;
That she could understand, like ships in port
And flowers in bloom. What need had folks of words?

With a great key that turned hard in the lock
She opened up the chapel door; inside
The cold came round her from the unwarmed rock,
The chill of places where the dead abide
And that faint smell of death, to her no shock,
Met and surrounded her as with a tide.
She found the lantern, struck the trembling light,
Warmth touched her fingers, and a yellow glow
Bloomed like a flower for an instant bright
Before she prisoned it in glass, and so
With reverent hands she lowered it alight
Into the martyrs' sepulchre below.

Now Soeur Marie was with them. What sweet tones
Her little mouth must make to tell these things:
Her gray gown was a shadow on the stones,
Her great, white coiffe a soaring angel's wings.
Baud's faint light shivered on the martyrs' bones
Until they seemed to sway as censor swings.
Baud trembled now,—as many times before,
She saw her martyrs' bones bees in a hive,
And she, their keeper, living, could adore
The bleached white death that kept her soul alive.
They looked at her. Ma Soeur's lips moved once more:
"—Came here when she was eight,—she's sixty five."

New York Hotel

The fly was here before I was and he is very agile,
He owns the place and I am the interloper.
He loves the cigarette-burned carpet,
The drab and dirty curtains,
The pompous lamps,
And the cracked marble lintel.
He probably walked on the faces of the last inhabitants
While they were sleeping.
He is a city fly and knows how to put me down
By dodging my blows and coming back to sit on my wrist.
Like the taxi driver who overcharged me with a defiant grin
And wouldn't get out to remove my luggage,
The fly is insolent.
Tomorrow I'll leave him in possession
And he can worry the next tenant.
I'll be glad to be gone.

The Nun

When she had been a long time kneeling there,
Saying with silent lips an endless prayer;
Until the sun fell through the western pane,
Dying the floor with a long crimson stain,
　　　Like Christ's red blood;
When she had felt her limbs cold to the bone,
Cold as a kneeling saint carven from stone,
When the low candle light dazzled her eyes
So that her troubled mind saw Paradise,
　　　Bursting from bud;
When she who trembled once felt now secure,
Felt her black heart washed white; empty and pure—
A flight of twittering birds crossed the red glass,
Brought back the world and all wild joys that pass,
　　　In a dark flood.

76

ALISON BROWN (1899-1949)

On St. Louis Bay

Keeping close to the sandy shore of Minnesota Point we paddled down the bay, leaving the sunset behind us and heading toward a slowly darkening sky where great clouds were piled, purple and blue at the base and foaming white above. The bay was quiet except for little waves that were hardly more than swells. Only when we drifted we could hear them slap against the canoe and feel the rise and fall of the water. Along the Point the dark green pines were deepening to black, and red and white cottages stood out vividly in the half-light.

Then we turned about toward the sunset. Night was closing down behind us and the last of daylight lay ahead. A pale orange band stretched above the darkening hills. Tiny lights began to appear, outlining the streets of the city. From the base of the hills white mist arose and trailed upward. Tall elevators loomed black in the pale golden light.

Other canoes slipped silently by, and voices came to us from the cottages on the shore. A sailboat passed us, distinct in every detail, but soon to become wraithlike in the dusk. A creaking rowboat labored by, a little girl at the oars, and in its stern a woman with a baby in her arms. One of the two children kneeling in the bow chanted softly, "Starbright, starlight," and looking upward we found the first pale star of the evening.

We gazed back over the way we had come, and above the pine trees far down the Point saw the rim of a great August moon. Soon it rose into full sight, lovely like a Japanese print, with a bank of gray clouds above it and an outspread branch outlined across its golden surface.

SISTER MARIS STELLA (1899–1987)

Grapes

Then there were the grapes turned purple in the sun
hanging in heavy bunches close and low.
These were great purple garden grapes. Not one
of the children had ever seen any but wild grapes grow.
Wild-running grapes are tart and spare and small.
You find the vines on big trees, clinging high
to withered branches, or on the sun-facing wall
of an old farmhouse. Invariably they lie
well out of reach, and tempting, and you find
gooseberry patches near them, and you gather
berries in buckets. Here you had no mind
to gather berries in buckets. Here you had rather
suck the sweet grapes out of their juicy blue
pockets and let the sun pour down on you.

I Who Had Been Afraid

I who had been afraid of the dark at night
as a child here in this room, even when I lay
safe by my mother's bed, now without fright
watched here alone until the break of day
my mother lying in the last sleep of all.
Never would she wake into the night again.
Here was the beautiful end. No child would call,
no grief disturb, no terrible, torturing pain
constrain her from the quiet. Here was at last
catharsis—all pity and terror spent.
Sorrow, splendor, living, dying—past.
All things fulfilled and nothing to lament.
I who had been afraid of the darkness, here
alone with the beloved dead found nothing to fear.

Riddles

Out of this tangle of threads to find the thread
that will untangle the threads. Out of the maze
to find the amazing path and so be led
back to the beginning by incredible ways.
Out of confusion of keys to find the key
that fits each keyhole, unlocks every lock.
Among a multitude of suns to see
only the sun. To find the moveless rock
under the shifting stones, under the sand,
the rock no shifting sands can ever shake,
nor great wind crying out over a shaken land,
nor lightning blast, nor breaking water break.
To find in multiplicity but one
end, beginning, thread, path, key, rock, sun....

Meridel LeSueur (1900–1996)

Rites of Ancient Ripening

I am luminous with age
In my lap I hold the valley.
I see on the horizon what has been taken
What is gone   lies prone   fleshless.
In my breast I hold the middle valley
The corn kernels cry to me in the fields
                    Take us home.
Like corn I cry in the last sunset
Gleam like plums.
                    My bones shine in fever
Smoked with the fires of age.
Herbal, I contain the final juice,
Shadow, I crouch in the ash
                    never breaking to fire.
Winter iron bough
                    unseen my buds,
Hanging close I live in the beloved bone
Speaking in the marrow
                    alive in green memory.
The light was brighter then.
Now spiders creep at my eyes' edge.
I peek between my fingers
                        at my fathers' dust.
The old stones have been taken away
                    there is no path.
The fathering fields are gone.
The wind is stronger than it used to be.
My stone feet far below me grip the dust.
I run and crouch in corners with thin dogs.

Fold in my flesh
      in future summers.
My body a canoe turning to stone
Moves among the bursting flowers of men.
Through the meadows of flowers and food,
I float and wave to my grandchildren in the
Tepis of many fires
            In the winter of the many slain
I hear the moaning.
I ground my corn daily
In my pestle many children
Summer grasses in my daughters
Strength and fathers in my sons
All was ground in the bodies bowl
     corn died to bread
        woman to child
          deer to the hunters.
Sires of our people
Wombs of mothering night
Guardian mothers of the corn
Hill borne torrents of the plains
Sing all grinding songs
     of healing herbs
Many tasselled summers
        Flower in my old bones
        Now.
Ceremonials of water and fire
Lodge me in the deep earth
   grind my harvested seed.
The rites of ancient ripening
Make my flesh plume
And summer winds stir in my smoked bowl.
Do not look for me till I return
       rot of greater summers
Struck from fire and dark,
Mother struck to future child.

I tie myself to the children like a kite.
I fall and burst beneath the sacred human tree.
Release my seed and let me fall.
Toward the shadow of the great earth
                let me fall.
Without child or man
                                I turn   I fall.
Into shadows,
        the dancers are gone.
My salted pelt stirs at the final warmth
Pound me death
        stretch and tan me death
Hang me up, ancestral shield
        against the dark.
Burn and bright and take me quick.
Pod and light me into dark.

Are those flies or bats or mother eagles?
I shrink   I cringe
Trees tilt upon me like young men.
The bowl I made I cannot lift.
All is running past me.
The earth tilts and turns over me.
I am shrinking
        and lean against the warm walls of old summers.
With knees and chin I grip the dark
Swim out the shores of night in old meadows.
Remember   buffalo hunts
Great hunters returning
Councils of the fathers to be fed
Round sacred fires.
The faces of profound deer who
                gave themselves for food.
We faced the east the golden pollened
        sacrifice of brothers.
The little seeds of my children
        with faces of mothers and fathers
Unbud me now
Unfurl me now
Flesh and fire
                burn
            requicken
                Death.

MARTHA OSTENSO (1900-1963)

She Who Brings Winter

The old, bitter witch,
　　　She is older now,
　　　Bitterer now,
And she carries a longer, stronger switch
　　　From a crookeder witch-tree bough.

The mean green eye of the old bitter witch
　　　Is meaner still,
　　　Is greener still,
Than it was when she hid with the toad in the ditch
　　　From the June moon high on the hill.

The hateful black tooth of the old bitter witch
　　　Is more full of hate,
　　　Say the star-folk, of late,
And they pretend it's because of a bowlful of rich
　　　Elf pudding she stole and she ate.

The old, bitter witch
　　　Is older now,
　　　Is colder now,
For the toad and the elves and the floating moon
Have gone to a place where it's always June,
And the land that they left will be dying soon
　　　'Neath the switch of the witch-tree bough.

The Farmer's Wife

He will not hear the cuckoo call,
The last faint snow will seal his eyes.
I shall see a lone star fall
Above the bare pine ere he dies.

My own heart and the clock will soon
Alone keep all the silence here—
Unless the foolish, crying loon
Or the chanting wind come near.

He will not hold the soil again
In his two hands, nor will his face
Lift to the power of the rain
That early April brings this place.

To the south his orchard lies,
His naked wheat-field to the west.
And well will *they* know when he dies
He loved me only second best.

The Fisherman

Then after all my fishing in the sea
With yellow, yellow nets of maiden's hair
For fishes finical, of ivory
And tortoises beshaded and ghost-rare,

I draw my nets and draw them like a strand
Of silken shine from out the watery light,
And loop them in across the winking sand
And weave of them a gloamy mantle bright

As sun-stones lying in a little pool
And looked upon by the first whitening star.
And now I wander inland where the cool
Calms of dew upon the evening are,

For fishes in the sea are silver-cold
And silver-pale as shavings of the moon,
And I would have a little thrush to hold,
And I would hear a little thrush's tune.

CARLETON WINSTON (1900-1989)

Seven Years Ago

Just so—this time—seven years ago,
Among tall grasses and sweet clover,
I lay and watched the clouds pass over
The green mounds, and the shadows throw
Their ancient patterns on the grass.
All this I saw, and laughed, and thought,
I shall be very lovely caught
In his warm arms, and I shall pass
Out of their reach knowing that soon
We shall lie quiet and alone,
Together in the moonlight grown
More shining in our bridal room.

And the old servant from the house
Came down and said, "It's growing late."
She stayed and let her tongue create
A mass of horror, let it carouse
Among queer twisted bits of steel
And come upon a man who lay
More broken than the steel. Her gray
Eyes glittered and could not conceal
The urgency of frightful tales.
She proudly held her old white head
And told of Norseland brides just wed
Who lost their lovers in sea gales.

Then she was gone, like an old witch
Among the shades, and I remained
And numbly counted cars, and strained
My eyes into the darkness which
Was stretching greedy fingers down
The road. The dampness of the night
Drew on the grass, the pink and white

Wet clover lay a pall upon
Dead things. Could I have dreamed, for we
Were sitting in the candlelight,
The witch a servant in starched white
Who smiling served our jubilee?

So fair we lay within that bed,
Such pure, dear warmth of human need,
We, the children of God indeed,
For in ourselves there had been spread
The sacrament of fierce sweet love.
And we lay shyly in our peace,
Senses exalted in release,
Our prayer sent out beyond, above.

Sweet clover is upon the air
And I lie waiting as before,
He dead, I living. All the more
I must be waiting here with care!

Edris Mary Probstfield (1907–1980)

A Penny For Your Thoughts

I'm watching that tree over there on the edge of the lake,
Throwing its shadowed silhouette against the sky,
Flame penciled in the lightning flashes,
Grim and silent always.
It must be grand to be a tree;
I wonder how many millions of things that tree knows
And keeps to herself?—
One woman who does not talk.
The dead limbs are wisest
For they are the most silent.
They have no leaves to whisper and chatter.
I wish I were that tall, black tree
With thoughts of my own.

L'envoi

Draw the curtains close, Marie, I'm tired of visiting.
Tell the people, please to go away.
If they've liked my songs a bit, or found my pictures fair,
I'd like to have them come again some day.

Stir the fire, please, Marie, and put the kettle on.
Strange, but I'm as tired as I can be.
I guess we're growing old, my dear, yes your hair's greying too.
We're two old women sitting down to tea.

Marion Thompson van Steenwyk
(1907-1976)

Autumn

I have a sense today of the year's dying,
A wise, old woman's sense of dying being a good thing.
A clairvoyant vision behind serene eyes,
Telling me that people are grateful for the year's end,
As old women are grateful for death,
Without knowing why;
But feeling a release from the too bright sun,
The too warm days, the too wide sky,
And quick life everywhere,
And being glad that they can withdraw again,
Into themselves.

Quietness

Quieter than sun's setting,
Quieter than the slow dropping of night,
And great wings folding,
So quiet is the heart that hoped all day
And all day waited.
So quiet, so tender,
Lest the feeble flame go out,
Lest death engulf it,
Lest tomorrow's sun never rise,
So quiet is the heart that hoped all day
And all day waited.
As quiet as the first star
That noiselessly comes through the dark.

Irene Paull (1908–1981)

To Bill Heikkila, American

WHOM THEY TRIED TO MAKE A MAN WITHOUT A COUNTRY;
GIVEN AT HIS FUNERAL IN SAN FRANCISCO, MAY 10, 1960

I am the wind
I am the northern wind that blows across the Arrowhead to you,
    Bill Heikkila
Across the land of ten thousand lakes
And the big sea waters.
I am the wind that whines in the open pits of Nashwauk and
    Hibbing and Coleraine
And blows upon the red dust of the Mesaba
I am the wind in the hoarse voices of the ships at Allouez,
    Duluth, Split Rock and Castle Danger
And all the ports of call of the Unsalted Sea.
You've heard me purring in the birches of the Big Fork, the Gun
    Flint and Echo Trails
Over the bunkhouses of the lumberjacks
I am the same wind that howled like a wounded wolf on the
    winter prairies.
I come to you bearing the perfume of the first spring crocus
The buds of lilacs
I come stroking the grey fur of the pussywillows.
I am the wind that breathes your father's name in the
    underground coal pits of Hanna, Wyoming
In the blast furnaces of the Monongehala
As I shall breathe your name forever in the Arrowhead
You live, Bill Heikkila, you live.
You live in the timbers of the mine shafts
You live in the rock between the furrows
You live in the stumps of cedar
And burnt over popple
On the road you cut to the Pale Face River.
The land nourishes men and men nourish the land
You have seeped to the roots of Minnesota
Like the melted snows of fifty-four winters.
I shall breathe your name, Bill Heikkila, among the jackpine
I shall mingle your dust with the red ore of the Mesaba

And where the long boats load at Allouez
And the fog horn warns them off the rocks of Castle Danger.
I am the wind that carried your shouts
I have spread them like pollen.
I am the wind that lifted your banners
I have scattered their seed
They shall blossom again on city streets
In another season.
You live, Bill Heikkila, you live
I am the Northern wind.

Wall Street Honors The Unknown Soldier

With heads bent low and bowed with grief
Upon your grave we lay this wreath.

Well, things are looking up this spring,
The market's really taken wing;
We ought to see a handsome boom
With plenty of scratch and elbow room.

He gave the most a man can give,
He died that other men might live.

Man, what a haul in '17!
We took the fat an' we took the lean,
Just chicken feed...all said and done,
To what we took in '41!
U.S. Steel just hit the sky,
And Bethlehem went plenty high;
Republic Iron and Steel was soaring
And Standard Oil was really pouring!

Who knows, perhaps he had a wife
Who mourned the passing of his life.

American Sugar waxed fat and sleek,
Railway Steel Spring hit a peak;
American Can sold pretty dear
And New York banks hit a record year.

How happy the little wife must be
To know he died for liberty!

Net earnings on capital stock were bright,
And foreign trade reached an all-time height;
Wheat went over three bucks a shot,
But a dollar was all the farmer got!

How proud his mother must have been!
(This time we really muscle in!)

These babies know we have our price,
The Dutch East Indies would be nice,
The British held the field enough,
Their customers will like our stuff.

How proud to know the son she bore
Gave all he had to end all war!

Greenland's an important base,
And Turkey's a strategic place;
One thing cannot be overlooked:
If peace breaks out, our goose is cooked!
Our brand-new arms would go untested;
Good God! The dough we've got invested!
The crash would wipe us off the map
With all these orders in our lap.

Without the hope of fame or booty,
This noble son has done his duty.

We've got to make our soldiers frisky,
Less chocolate sodas and more whisky;
To dominate the Chinese yen,
Is worth a couple million men.
We need more bodies if this will be
The Great American Century.

And so we honor you, the dead,
And lay this wreath upon your head;
With silent prayer...be with us yet.
Lest we forget...lest we forget.

GERALDINE ROSS (1910–1995)

Love Potion

This subtle witchery is not
Exclusively of honey pot
Or dainty distillation of
A lilac spray. White-hot is love
And dangerous and kind and mad.
Take a wedge of shadow. Add
Anything of dream that sleep,
Gray, elusive, let's you keep;
Add a color, violent,
Red, perhaps. Take merriment
Trembling on the edge of pain,
Take a mumbled curse, the stain
Of sun through purple glass where light
Combines with piety. Take white,
The most complete that you can find,
Snow, linen, or a holy mind.
Boil and stir and pour and serve,
You will get what you deserve.
Fate's hand, guiding, will not stop.
Drink! Drink to the last bright drop!

Three A.M.

I might as well be all alone in space.
No one could warm or comfort one who lies
Staring at darkness with too-knowing eyes,
Remembering no friendly voice or face.
All love and hate are unimportant now,
As though I had already died. I touch
The tumbled comforter, my own cool brow,
In case I have—not that it matters much.
Some vivid, stubborn part of my own mind
Insists that I shall dance, shall hold love dear,
Shall wake to find both light and living kind,
Frail music fainting past the straining ear!
What must I learn that I should long have known?
Why must I lie so utterly alone?

Betty Bridgman (1915-1999)

The Tire Swing

Winter-long against the snow
The black tire swing kept saying O.
Whenever you looked out over the sink,
there it hung like the missing link
from autumn past to spring ahead,
and O was all it ever said.

Sometimes motionless, hanging plumb,
sometimes blown like a pendulum,
ticking the days and months away
with "zero" registered every day—
till now the roots of the elm tree show,
and children run, and the big black O
has a pair of corduroy legs put through
and all the summer it's saying Q.

Letter of Introduction

To whichever rivers it may concern:
        I send you my son of seventeen
to wade your waterfalls and learn
to find the portage, to paddle stern
        where you run cold and clean.

Float him north to the north I know:
        backwater lilies, tamarack,
haven where mother mallards go
with twenty young ones in a row,
        counting, keeping track.

Scrape all night on island shore
        where he flattens lavender aster petals.
Fill up his canvas pail and pour
part of the water he must explore
        into his sooty kettles.

Take him, rivers, run white and fast
out of your forest, out of my past.

Lucille Broderson (b. 1916)

Letter Never Sent

This letter is about me, the real me, the mother
you've never met. The one you invite to dinner
on Christmas or Easter or the birthday is an imposter.
Or perhaps you already know, then this
will be no surprise. But you'll act surprised
and hug me hard when next we meet. "Oh, no,"
you'll say, "you're not like that at all. Not at all!"
Because you, like the me you know, have been trained well.

But back to me. I lied.
"Lied." A strong word, an honest word.
I did not have a father, that's true.
It's true, he died. I was a child then, almost ten.
"Oh, how she loved him, how she misses him!"
But I never missed him. Why should I miss him?
I found another...at the library, in the Elsie Dinsmore book.
He meant business, that father.
No! No! Do this! Do that.
And I did it all. Right. How pleased Mother was.
How lucky her friends said—a child that is no trouble.

I grew up, not tall, not pretty but pretty enough
and a young man wanted me.
He was as good a father to me as the book father...
found the house, paid the bills, ordered the children,
cared for me, loved me, he said, but I never believed.
He died too. Too soon, of course, but he left me
"well enough off": my own home, my car, my bankbook.
But I never loved him. Nor the man who followed him.

Then one day I woke and knew I hated the world,
the people in it, the books that stood every which way
on my shelves, the pages I'd written, the pillows on my bed,
the flowers on the table, the bare trees out my window,
the wide snow-covered lake.

And I knew I never loved anything or anyone
but you, my children. Forgive me, but it's true.

Ruth F. Brin (b. 1921)

September

Autumn will come. How shall I celebrate this solemn term?
I think: according to the custom of the worm.
Ignorant as it of wings and flight
I will crawl upward to some unscaled height
and wrapped in silk secretions there, not knowing
whether bright wings, all cramped and hid, are growing;
whether I'll live, emerge and change, or if I'll die,
like an old leaf next spring, crumbling and dry;
I'll wait, like that green caterpillar there
wrapped tight in threads of self-secreted prayer.

Mary A. Pryor (b. 1926)

Oranges

When winter ratchets down its crunch-bone cold, oranges
provide our talisman, our bough of gold, oranges.

They are not rare, as in our parents' shared anecdotes,
exotic gifts a stocking toe might hold, oranges.

Thin-skinned and rich in oils, blue-ribbon specimens,
perfume the fingertips when palmed and rolled, oranges.

Girdled by four equators, pared meticulously,
eight petals curl, disclose the pulp, unfold oranges.

Segments divide, cathedral window-stained translucency
bursts on the tongue; heart hungers are consoled, oranges.

Papaya, mango, carabóla, persimmon
forsworn, we load the cargo bay with cold oranges.

Let the Olympians brag their nectar, their ambrosia.
Our feast is not less rightfully extolled, oranges.

Barefoot, we trod where warm waves wreathed our ankle bones
and bobbed with windfalls. From those waves we trolled oranges.

Make no mistake. Such food as feeds and cheers is luxury,
however cheap or dear or freely doled: oranges.

Indentured pickers work for pittance. Little changes
since wenches hawked, by stage-lamp, bawdy-bold, oranges.

What renders living graciously exploitative:
the justice-lover moralistic scold? Oranges?

Thus cries the roving minstrel, "Sweet or sour or contraband—
come buy my wares, if you can be cajoled: oranges."

Joanne Hart (b. 1927)

Fish

Because I remember Grandfather tiny, old,
silent, obeying the white-haired matriarch,
my grandmother, I love this large photograph
of him with Daddy. Even here he's not
smiling, but looks strong, young with, perhaps,
a smile hovering under the moustache.

Daddy's ten years old, knee pants, suspenders,
bare feet, Huck Finn stance. From his right hand
a monster pickerel hangs, caught in the Minnesota
sweeping downstream past the family garden.
The boy grins, happy to make his father proud—
it's there in the way young Clarence grasps
his bamboo pole, face to the camera lens.

I heard no stories from Grandfather,
but lore of him as linguist came from Daddy
how John would close his barber shop
when Sioux, appearing at the door like shadows,
asked him to translate their dealings
with the Agent. He'd learned their tongue.
He went with them. They trusted him.
Today the same Sioux Band reels in
casino gamblers. Such big fish the Sioux
catch now would surely make Grandfather smile.

Phebe Hanson (b. 1928)

Cinderella

After your mother turns to stone,
you sit beside your father
in the high Model A,
driving to church in the country.
You sit in the front row,
singing hymns in Norwegian
to please him.

At home in the kitchen
you make Eggs Goldenrod
for him and your other children,
laughing as you blow crumbled yolks
at each other.

You are as good and as beautiful
as your mother.
Secretly you smile to yourself:
he needs no other wife.

When summer comes, you lie
aching and peeling with Scarlet Fever.
A hired woman brings you meals in bed.
You can go nowhere with him for weeks.

He heads his car away
from your quarantined house,
finds another to replace you.
Later, the new mother smiles
down at you from the high front seat,
while you climb into the back
with the other children.

Sacred Heart

In Sacred Heart, Minnesota,
we Lutherans
barely knew the Catholic kids.
Their mothers smoked Camels,
played bridge in the afternoons
instead of Ladies' Aid.
Their fathers, lying under their Chevvies,
said, *goddamn*, cursing the motors to life.

But we build bird baths of cement,
pressed splinters of broken bottles
into their wet breasts.
Hosiery salesmen driving through
to the Cities marveled.

We gave hoboes
who asked at our backdoors for food
glasses of buttermilk
because it was good for them.

When I was eight, a big Catholic kid asked me
up to his garage loft to see his crucifix.
Even then I knew that the Lutherans are justified
by faith alone,
and kept my legs crossed.

Sturdy Arms

"You've got sturdy arms," my blind date said,
a student from Norway studying to be a missionary
to Madagascar. I was pretending to study English Lit,
but really on the alert at all times for a suitable husband.

"You'd make a good worker out on the mission field,"
my date went on. I stood on the steps of Sivertsen Hall,
Augsburg College, a few blocks from where the Mississippi
River flowed past to the University of Minnesota.

That's where I should have gone, I thought, where I'd meet
atheists and agnostics, studying to get rich some day, and when
I married one, he'd hire cleaning women so I could sit for hours
in my room, my sturdy arm writing poem after poem after poem.

Carol Connolly (b. 1934)

Shallows

For the 577 demonstrators
arrested at Honeywell
on October 23, 1984

I want to float in the shallow water
close to the shore
where the sea is still,
the sand is white.

I want to loll
on my back on a puffed-up life raft,
search for the silver lining,
gaze at the sky as blue as blue,

glide straight into the sun,
and be consoled.
Never look back.
I have been in deep water.

I could
tell you stories
you would not
believe.

I will be alone now,
solitary, celibate.
I don't want to hear even a whisper
of the syllables in *nuclear,*

the hiss in *holocaust,*
the murder in *mutilation.*
I don't want to smell the sweat
in *demonstrate* or *lobby* or *elect.*

The kingfishers will roar by
in speedboats.
I won't even wave.
Far in the distance
the heat shimmers.
You may decide
to board a big boat,
chain your body to a war machine.

Remove all sharp objects
from your pockets
so you won't hurt yourself
or wound the cop who arrests you.

The steel door will bang behind you.
The jailor will say your time begins.
Keep in mind,
what is legal is not,

and as you pour strength
into the deep ocean
that floats my raft close to the shore,
I will be safe in the sun
because you
hold back the dark
with your bare hands.

Edith Rylander (b. 1935)

Too Good to Waste

Mid-summer and humid, it must have been near 90
When you called up, "Edie, have you any spare canning rings?"
And I carried them uphill
Under trees losing their last light

To the house full of grandkids' pictures,
And you laughing
Over two five-gallon buckets and a galvanized tub
Of cucumbers—from your garden, from my garden, from
    some other lady's,
All given at once,
"Too good to waste."

All this before the cancer;
All this before the house went up for sale.

And we worked together, scrubbing, sorting, brining, washing jars,
Fitting lids, in that steamy kitchen,
Noses prickling with vinegar and spice,
Mopping our faces

Till the last jar sealed, and we sat in the sticky dark
Of midnight, drinking coffee,
So tired we were silly.

Cooling jars ticked in the kitchen.
Downhill, grebes chattered
On the dark lake,

And you sang me "Nikolina" in Swedish,
Stopping between verses
To let me know what was going on.
"This young fellow goes to meet the farmer's daughter,
But the farmer hits him with a big stick."

Laughing, singing words
In your birth language
That I don't know:

"Then they decide they'll wait to get together
Till the old man dies.
This is not a very respectable song."

Jill Breckenridge (b. 1938)

Jacob, Crossing Over

If you'd cross over the great Ohio,
first try to find her frozen, then
remember these names to meet your freedom:
Cairo   Evansville   Leavenworth
They may ride you down first, their dogs
tear off your wet clothes, and when you're
stripped, bend you over a barrel,
Madison   Rising Sun   Lawrenceberg
beat you all over your bare back
with a cobblestone paddle—its forty
holes—every hole drawing its own blister,
Cincinnati   New Richmond   Moscow
and then the Blacksnake whip, that stiff
handle, three feet of it, like a club,
and the lash, its snake mouth hissing,
Ripley   Manchester   Rome
or a cat-o'-nine tails, each one
doing its own work plowing up your back,
winding around your body, purring,
Portsmouth   Ironton   South Point
but whatever whip they choose,
they'll work it on you till every blister
breaks open, blood running down to your heels,
Burlington   Jeffersonville   Marietta
and then their salt-water wash,
strong enough to float a spoon in,
the salt and the blood and the screaming.
Wellsburg   Steubenville   Point Pleasant
But if you get there, the silence will be yours,
the trees, the earth, and the grass upon it,
the blue blue sky will be yours, all yours.
Proud to meet you, Master Freedom.

Will Sommers, Confederate Soldier

DECEMBER 30, 1862: THE NIGHT
BEFORE THE BATTLE HE PREPARES
TO FIGHT, GUN NOT LOADED.

To have risen before the black rooster,
myself crowing in the new day, to have heard
the chorus of wild birds blessing the dew
on my land, to have sunk my hands up to the wrists
in dirt, dark and warm as inside of a cow,
reaching for the turned strangling head of her new one,
to have touched the silky tassel of wheat, golden,
the newly shorn rug of a sheep's back,
the white oak plank I've sanded smooth,
soft as the inside of a woman's elbow,
stroked the underwater skin of catfish, cool
and dark, that surprise of spines, to have dropped
seed into holes I alone made, firmed
warm earth down around them, to have witnessed
the first green shoots, threads of life
so strong in their push for sun they cracked
apart the earth, to have fought squirrel, crow,
rabbit, drought, army worm, drought,
weevil, flood, despair, Hessian fly,
grasshopper, blight, cankerworm, despair,
to keep new life alive, to have watched the green
blades of young corn curl under,
brown like brittle fodder in the scorch of sun,
to have mourned the hay rotting on the ground in rain,
to have held the still warm calf I could not save,
shot the delicate bay mare
mired in the mud hole, half eaten by wild boar,
to have smelled my wife's hair, long
and darkly sweet, new washed, drying in the sun,
to have caught, with my rough hands, a daughter,
then two sons and held them, heard them, slippery
red, cry out their first hellos, to have built
a tiny box from the old cedar, buried a girl,
fist no bigger than a plum,
to have watched my wife's face, a full year
vacant as a winter pasture, to have smelled,

on the coldest day, the welcome warmth of urine and hay
from the just-opened barn door, returned
to the smell of coffee in the kitchen, fresh biscuit
and bacon, to have seen my wife's face slowly
brighten, her cheek regain its wild-rose blush
when I put my lips upon it, to have picked
and tasted the wild raspberry, sun-warmed,
sweet and sour as first dumb desire,
to have been partner with so much life,
to have lived this long, to have lived...

SHARON CHMIELARZ (B. 1940)

Another Love Letter
(AFTER SHARON OLDS)

Irene Hartland, Dad. You could have had her by the looks of this photo.
Nice legs. Her silk stockings glare in the sun.
She's interested—standing beside you, curving in. The other girl
(my mother) on the left is too nice. Forget her. Irene is the one.
She likes your tender bulk in that winter coat with its fur epaulets.
She likes the sweater you wear underneath, and the way the collar
stands up like a prince's ruff around the back of your neck.
Consider her name, Dad. "Deer land." You'll be reasonably happy.
She's a German Russian, too, she understands how to handle men like you.

No, not Irene? How about "Maggie?" or Miss Fay? Or Miss Moon?
Tête-â-teté in the photo, your arm around her, you're bending down,
your six feet toward her, a wicked, sexy grin on your clean-cut face.
Dad, stop right there. I'll go back to the universe and wait another round.
I herewith condemn my sisters to the same, we slide gladly out of the picture.
For you. For Vila Netz. Or the Billigmeier girl. Either of the Miller sisters.
They all have a crush on you, your sunglasses, round as quarters.
Remove us, your daughters, and you're a frat boy, a movie star,
advertiser, salesman, efficiency expert from 160 acres in North Dakota.

Not a plugger. Not the wild, crazy-eyed wife beater.
Look at you now!
You who would not listen. You are a big,
lumpy walrus, old, wearing a cap for the Sitting Bull Stampede.
Smiling because you've found three women who can live with you
underwater for an hour at a time. Your arms slide easily around us,
your daughters, your girls. Where you've taped this photo
into the album, I find two of your gray hairs. Two from the grave?
I almost pull them out, and then, realizing it's too late,
I let you be.

Florence Chard Dacey (B. 1941)

The Threshold

The whooping crane is an endangered species, brought back
from near-extinction by ingenious humans, but still in peril.

Over our subtle states of mind
the fine print
        the whooping crane
hesitates
        one foot
poised

            a precision instrument.

        A single crane
harbors
        vast isolate valleys
under her wings,
        rises like a rarified rig
from managed marshes
        where blue crabs so far still feed
her royal mauve
        feathers ruffling like
white sepulchres in fog

            sculpted clippers at the dawn.

        And the prow
the curve of that neck
        graced by wind's egress
lap of water on shell and egg
        that head we calculate in

our paltry arithmetic:

Fifty nesting pairs
would be
        enough, they say,
sufficient beaks and bones
        feathers
stern eyes enough
        to fly
to bear us
        over

                the threshold.

Diane Glancy (b. 1941)

American Miniaturist

She is
smaller than
history, her
acts of
childbirth not
recorded, her
acts of
obedience. How
severely she
is captured
by oil
paint on
a small
oval, hair
parted up
the middle,
tied behind
her head
to hold
her ears
open to
his voice,
which is
something like
a sidewalk
crusted after
sleet on
snow. Her
own voice
is a
pile of
leaves whose
tongues are

veined and
forked after
Indian wars,
stuffed into
the puppet
of her
mouth, a
sock-monkey twisted
and knotted
in a
shape not
its own.

Eva Hooker (b. 1941)

So Unlike Any Simple Thing I Know

Near the gray barn, the tumultuous sky
the color of white-bean ash:

it seems as if the lights of the truck
barreling through tunnels of white

do not blink, but strum the gravel
ragged along the road; it seems as if,

half sound, half silence, the sky
is composed to number and stay my wheels:

how long it takes to move round the curve
in the dark, careful like an empty freight

car: how the Schramel farm rises up,
unhurried, its exhausted fence too strong

to fall upon itself in the wind:
how sometimes at twilight you can see

the dead fall and the sun floating down
like bloodroot: how I have lived like that.

Mary Kay Rummel (b. 1941)

A Little Helper

That's what my mother wanted.
It was hot work. She wore print dresses
and told me to iron while my brothers ran
to the river with BB guns and hunting knives.
Their shirts, rolled like sausages, waited, damp
until the iron flattened them.

One week of shirts for five men,
iron, brick heavy, sprinkle
the water bottle, slap it down,
push steam ahead of it, travel
those wide cotton backs,
do the yokes without wrinkling,
the narrow sleeves.

The day her brother, Patrick, fell at work
Mother asked me to iron while she waited
at his bed. I dug through the pile for
the easiest shirts, then ran to the beach.

When her brother died
I drowned in her rage

over the ironing undone, the daughter
who was never a help, or helper, over
our unspoken loneliness as my brothers
slammed the door on their way in and out again.

Margot Fortunato Galt (b. 1942)

Relations

If you wonder why six women
pose in black gowns with some relief
of lace or jewel at the neck,
look at their faces: down-turned mouths,
staring eyes. The mothers behind
have fostered the daughters in front.
Fatherhood forgotten, they perch
at black-bird gravesites.
They ride the unsteady roofs
of houses in flood. Their skirts
shelter fears, dust
driven through walls, settling
a pall on clean linen,
grit in the mouth.

A descendent stoops to wipe
dirt from the floor.
Her baby cries. Vapor fills
rooms with their unmistakable
hands, clenching, relaxing.

They have collected buttons and string,
shards of skirt and apron
until their names are sewn crazy
across fields. I have known
six women to spend
hundreds of stitches
on a quilt that went to warm
a tractor in winter.

Susan Carol Hauser (b. 1942)

Acorn

Now you have the earth
firmly beneath your feet.
At eighteen months you can even run,
paying no attention to where
you are going. Only the acorns
in the driveway bring you
to consideration. They have taken
their seasonal place among the pebbles
that all the summer long
you claimed as yours.
We had learned to watch
for the quick move of your
hand to mouth, and to know
what it was your lips
closed on as though on a secret.

Give me the stones, we'd say,
and you learned to let them go,
released into a proffered hand,
dropping like coins from a slot machine.

No one saw the acorn go in, but in
the house when you tried to answer
the question I gave to you, I saw it
rolling in there, wet and shiny,
the brown nearly amber with the polish
you'd been giving it.

You let it go into my hand
but I understand the call
of acorns and we returned
to the driveway and you bent
knees and waist and harvested
by the handful. I showed you
the pocket in your Levis
and one by one you placed the acorns
into the slot, then kept
your hand there, rolling them
as though on your tongue, accepting
the kiss of their mute promise.

Martha George Meek (b. 1942)

Saint Stranger

In the cave below the great cave
of the church, Father Wilfred
opens the reliquary up
to our curiosity. He knows its secrets
won't disperse before the gaze
of visiting scholars; neither will they
let us be. A dozen vases wink
from niches in the walls. He empties one,
and slivers of bone spill into my palm.
Here's hard evidence, but of what?
Wilfred doesn't even say
whose bones. He's at home with the sacred,
like the old monk wearing
bedroom slippers upstairs in the nave.

We can just make out the skeleton
under the glass floor of the altar.
No one is sure of this saint's *bona fides*:
the small martyr Peregrine, meaning
stranger, translated from Rome
to Minnesota. What does it matter,
skeletons don't have names.
Some abbey faxed they have a bone,
Wilfred says mildly, but he's all there.

Beneath a gauze veil, rows
of red glass beads are pasted
on the skull for eyebrows. Glass beads
overflow the sockets of the face,
lodge between the big, horse teeth.
Homely and exotic ornaments,
they paint a face of longing, whether
for life or death, I can't tell.

Under the altar, there's nothing left
of the battered child. Our skeletons
all look the same. Only the narrow shoulders
make a pathetic claim. Otherwise,
here lies the terrifying idea of us.
Once, I saw the abbey potter in his workshop
lift his girl's arm to the light
while she stood like the statue
of a dancer. He said, her bones and trees
are both alumina and silica:
evidence of the continuous creation
running through the veins of trees, our veins,
our bones, the clay, and the bowl the potter
shapes. I've watched him at his wheel,
how with his thumbs he coaxes roundness
from the clay. Secrets cluster around
his gestures, pool, and settle in the cup.

Wilfred wonders will I write about *him*;
I don't know. I don't know how long I remain
by the Stranger, humming to hear the bones ring:
incus, malleus, stapes. I watch
the dry chest rise and fall
in steady breathing, an old trick
of my eyes that makes stars jump.
Leaving here, I'll trace the slow
course of the potter's metaphor.
I, too, am bone, thank God.
The secret's inside me. I can afford to be
infinitely patient; I'll have it with me
when I go.

Monica Ochtrup (b. 1942)

Alone

I knew it very early, at the age of four or five, and the morning
was a summer morning like this one. I went through the screened
porch and onto the steps outside where I sat playing with a set of
toy dishes made of cobalt blue glass. The color of the glass was
deeply satisfying. That, and at the same time filled me with
a terrible longing. I can remember the moment when I stopped
playing with the dishes and lifted one of the small glasses, cut
with facets that deepened the blue, and held it—not up to the
light—but on the open palm of my hand: wanting. That blue and
the glass made me want, not the glass itself, but something that
the glass was. I put it down and began to walk up and down the
sidewalk in front of our house. The sidewalk was empty and the
blue glass was back on the steps in among the other dishes. I knew
it was no use to go back to the dishes. Then I thought: If I had a
friend, if a friend and I played with the dishes—but suddenly I
knew it would not help this. Whatever the blue glass satisfied
and made me long for, playing with a friend was not part of it. I
stopped walking then, and chose a spot on the front lawn where I
lay down on my back, looking up into the heavily leaved branches
of the great elm growing on the boulevard and reaching over
above me, making a deep shade. Through the branches I could
see the sky, and from the small of my back I knew: alone.

NANCY PADDOCK (B. 1942)

Bombers

1

It's wide open back of the houses.
Kids I don't know are playing a big kid game
I try to play, but don't understand.
It is 1945, I'm not quite three.
Mama and I wait for the war to end
and Daddy to come home.

Black planes roar overhead and the boys yell,
Bombers! Bombers! They dive
like rabbits into the bushes,
all part of their game.
I don't know bombers,
but I crouch small
inside the lilacs, Chicken Little afraid
of the sky.

2

It is night in Falmouth, England, just before D-Day;
my father lies in a hedgerow.
Luftwaffe bombers strafe. Antipersonnel bombs
fall to thirty feet above his head,
spraying death.

Living to tell the story, my father said,
I finally got fatalistic—after
I'd said the 23rd Psalm: The Lord
is my shepherd, I shall not want... *I turned over*
and looked up
at the biggest fireworks display ever.

3

Fifty years later on the Fourth of July,
inside a houseboat at Harriet Island,
my father is silent.
Up on deck, they are oohing and ahhing
at the patriotic display.

But my father's eyes are closed.
He makes himself small in the chair
as if the sky is falling.

MADELON SPRENGNETHER (B. 1942)

Lot's Wife

FOR MONA VAN DUYN

You saw it so clearly, that terrible moral of punishment and
shame. How the men, nervous and obsessed, worry over
judgment, when the gist of the story lies elsewhere   the legacy of
a woman with no name. Who should care which organ goes into
which orifice, the sum of humiliation or sorrow, who did what to
whom? The angels, those honored guests, would sacrifice anyone
to save themselves. A crime worse than you would have believed.
This is what caused you to mourn, relinquishing your own hopes
and wishes. Someone, you felt, should pay respect to the flawed,
perishable, human past.

CARY WATERMAN (B. 1942)

After the Pig Butchering
> "WHAT DOES THE PIG THINK OF THE DAWN?
> THEY DO NOT SING BUT THEY HOLD IT UP."
>
> —PABLO NERUDA

I go back two days later
for the skin.
It is dismal weather.
The floor of the shed is wet
where blood mingles with the red paint
and the dark soft manure.
It is a watercolor of confusion and pain,
of the loss of a piece of thought.
The feeding pans are in chaos,
tipped like crazy men around the corners.

I have come back to pick up the skin.
We left the entrails to droop in a compost heap.
I see them sinking like heat into the ground.
I know parts of them are ovaries.
And there are two blue-lipped stomachs
that seem to smile at me.
The skin is on the roof of the shed.

Carrying it I can tell that it weighs
about as much as my five-year-old son.
It is solid like a head against my breasts.
I begin to like carrying it and squeeze it closer,
rub my cheek into it,
and touch the taut nipples.
They are watchtowers
on both sides of the river we cut open
I am bringing it home.

Now the smell is on me,
grease on my hands.
I bring it all into my house.
It slides around the doors,
under the beds.
It is pungent
and obsessive.

Me Learning To Dance

I don't know how.
And so you pose before me,
a right angle, a cock-eyed telephone pole
ready to begin.

Mother watches, approving.
She is tiny.
I am tiny.
And you are so much bigger,
weaving like Goliath
in the space before me.

And then we start this strangeness,
bobbing and heaving like heavy ducks.
Right, left,
right, right, left.
You going one way,
me following like an afterthought.
Steam swirls from our heads
as we circle the small room
ten minutes before my date arrives.

But it is too late.
Here he is with a corsage box,
two tiny pink tea roses squeezed
by the gregarious carnations.
And I go off with him into the night,
into his car.

And I do not love him.
It is you I love.
But I never tell you,
never tell you,
never.

Patricia Barone (b. 1943)

Last Night On a Northern Lake

FOUR CURTAL SONNETS FOR AN ALZHEIMER'S PATIENT

1

The loon doesn't laugh when it snares
a mackerel, but only when fishing
without catching the merest minnow.
From dives that slide beneath the water,
it pops up, slick pinions dripping
but empty beak. The loon, its yodeled

prat-call, is for Alice, who collects
clues of her former life—some morsels, *things*,
She laughs—ha HA, ha HA! and sinks below
the medicine cart—a useless life raft—
the P.M. nurse's purview.

2

At its empty plate, the moon's white face,
the loon guffaws hoo ah! Alice startles.
The table of the loon is set with blue
spruce around the lake's wind-wrinkled waves,
with silver salt cellars, Hungarian dark
pepper falling on the oval eggs the loon

broke while laying. The yolks look cross-eyed
at Alice, who locates her hunger near her heart,
who searches for the one cake she must have,
must swallow to grow smaller, crawl inside
her old house, be saved.

3

The crumbs of the loon's cold dinner
are fish eggs, then minnows—they swim away
from Alice. She wades the hall to salvage any little
words (and steals the nurse's pen): loon-like wandering,
her head held lower than her wings. Her feet ache;
she cannot stay, she only takes. One ankle is

name-banded so she can't escape. Hee oooh! (like a moan)
laughs Alice, her solo at the home, and she breaks free.
A chorus of ululations—rising on the weather's
changing, from inlet, shore, fen—each sound alone.
On their wind current,

4

Her mattress moves out upon the water in the wake
of a loon's high chortle, and so many name brands
that she can't use or place are bobbing in the tow-tide.
Husband, children, grandchildren—all stand upon the dock
too far away. Alice must housekeep the flotsam and jetsam—
keys, sweaters, scraps of paper, bowls, and fedoras.

Let things go, let them sink beneath the under wing
coverts and the upper wing cross-striped coverts
and the sleek green head of the loon, as Alice drifts
and covets through her dream—the loon's gleaming
blue neck band.

Nancy Fitzgerald (B. 1943)

Arrival: 1973

"Why must your adopted daughter
be Korean?" the social worker asked.
Faces floated before me:
girls with bangs, bobbed hair,
close cropped to the crown,
walking to school in uniforms
white blouses, navy skirts.
I saw them in my dreams,
standing on swing seats,
pumping higher than the kids at home,
jumping rope, following the taffy man
who clacked his giant shears calling them
to buy rice candy cut from clear thin sheets.
I saw them every time an Asian child passed,
and I wanted one. "Because I lived there
as a child," I said. "I grew to love the people
and the Land of Morning Calm."

While we worked through immigration
waiting, waiting for bureaucrats
she stayed in foster care. For eight months
I was pregnant, alone in my own body,
measuring the way to Seoul,
measuring how she grew: now her teeth
are coming in, now she babbles, eats rice cakes,
walks, laughs, and bonds to others she will miss.
She was not smiling in her picture on our fridge,
scowling in her cotton padded vest,
waiting to come West to Northern light,
to find her place in a family constellation
she had no choice about.

A thousand silver cranes took flight
beside the plane which carried her.
When they placed her in my arms
I felt a stirring in my womb.
More treasured than a sack of rice,
awaited like spring rain.
A thousand silver cranes took flight,
and they have settled here.

Norita Dittberner-Jax (b. 1944)

The Feast of the Holy Family

And here they are!
Three generations of the same nose,
streaming toward the baggage carousels
to a jazzy "Hark! The Herald," good
flying weather and the holiday over.

Again at curbside pick up,
families gather and separate
and gather again, talking cell phone
to cell phone, parents tugging
their children back from the happiness

of no school tomorrow, a Smart Carte
weaves between the Somalis, so
tall and elegant, jocks huddle
around the afternoon's win,
the cleaner steers

the mountain of refuse, our steadfast
overindulgence. The Muzak
shifts to "The Hallelujah Chorus,"
played by three brass and a kazoo,
it's tinny, it's tawdry,

the suitcases bounce
down the hold
the family
home and safe.
Hallelujah!

Julie Landsman (b. 1944)

Laos on the Radio

Driving home on Minnehaha, past a garden shop full of
Christmas evergreens, where just months ago geraniums
collected scarlet and purple sunlight, I flip the
radio from jazz to news: a story about Laos.

> *One Laotian child dies every day as he stumbles on a mine*
> *buried in the fields, or resting in the open, or nestled in*
> *hills near the village.*

Last year in third hour, Hmong students from Laos
wrote of hills in the gray scrim of a wet dawn, of
green land and blue mountains, water and hard farming.
They told me of their grandfathers in the cool
morning, hovering over poppies: red blossoms against
black pants, white smocks; "Laos is like a dream. How
much our mothers want to return!"

> *But one man struggles up the terraced gardens to show*
> *fathers and mothers how to search for leftover explosives,*
> *an American legacy hidden in trees and rocks, grass and*
> *flowers. With large and knowledgeable fingers he helps*
> *farmers break apart cylinders, clocks, metal triggers. They*
> *all work together in monsoon green. Yet no one man, no*
> *one uncle can be on each dirt path, near each river, on the*
> *edge of each mountain, all the time.*

I turn onto Lake, the car rocking with chill wind. I
remember Mai Nhia, Mai Yer, Pa Yang in front of me at
dawn last November, my classroom windows opening to
cold light. Their slim fingers sorted lunch money as
they spilled words full of vowels to each other before
the first bell. I am suddenly grateful that all these
children still wake to this shivering winter.

In the very hills their mothers ache for,

a little girl crawls from her sister's side, stretches her small arms toward something that glitters in morning light, a treasure of red metal...

Roseann Lloyd (b. 1944)

Natt og Dag: Return To Norway After 25 Years

I wanted to know the names of things,
words I'd forgotten, words I'd never learned
the first time: the name of the tiny violet,
for instance, snuggling in the crack
of the mossy boulder by the cabin.
A sunny gold face with a purple forehead,
purple hair.
           The two women disagreed
about its name. Eva said, *Its name is Dag*
og Natt, that's Day and Night. She should know—
she said, she'd been picking them ever since
she was a child. The other, Mette, said, *Oh, no,*
most definitely not. Its name is Natt
og Dag, because the night
is the mother of the day. Not the other way
around.
           They went back and forth.
Each stood her ground. At first I favored Eva's
childhood memory, being who I am. Impressed
that she sported fuchsia toenails—the exact match
to her shiny rain suit. And that she walked
barefoot in the rain—
all tan and fuchsia!
           But in the end
I had to go with Mette's naming,
being who I am. Because it pleased me.
Comforted me, even. Because I kept on
saying her words whenever I saw a dark purple
violet with a golden face... *Natt og Dag.*
Natt og Dag.   *Fordi natten*
er dagens mor.
           Because the night is
the mother of the day.

Freya Manfred (b. 1944)

Inside the Boat House

Inside the boat house
sunlight reflected off water
writes dappled messages
on the wooden walls.
Or perhaps it's not writing,
but a song,
soft notes cascading
like cathedral bells.
Or maybe it's
a kind of breathing:
in for darkness,
out for light.
Or, it might be
the fleeting touch
of an invisible lover's fingers:
nothing that can be read,
sung,
or breathed,

only felt,
upon the skin we share with day.

Mary Rose O'Reilley (b.1944)

The Foster Child

Weaving a basket of the day, they
who seldom spoke otherwise
talked in bed.

It was not a house for privacy:
two rooms and a sleeping porch;
I on my couch overheard
everything said.

Propped on pillows, he smoked a pipe,
she fingered rosary beads,
between them the basket was finished

and put aside in the methodical way
they did everything:
played cribbage, carted the leaves away.

No ideas hung on the blackberry vine
they wove into the warp of real things,
words for *mice, feathers,* and *wings,*

for the white cat who loved them,
birch trees and wrens.
A few feet from the door

the waves kept lapping.
I'd never been given before
a sense of containment,

and never got it again,
except I can weave it now on my own,
out of the talk and stillness of that home.

Patricia Hampl (b. 1946)

St. Paul: Walking

The old city of saints opens its hand again this morning,
      its claw of money and glass rosaries.
I never say no.
Together we have broken bread, promises, hearts,
      whatever drags beneath our muddy river.
I put my bare hand on the red stone of the millionaire's house:
      it sizzled like water in a black pan.
Sometimes I think I will hold forever the hand of this city;
      it shakes its fist of beer and greenhouses at me,
      its long death sways on the stem of an orchid even in winter.

The Moment

Standing by the parking-ramp elevator
a week ago, sunk, stupid with sadness.
Black slush puddled on the cement floor,
the place painted a killer-pastel
as in an asylum.
A numeral 1, big as a person,
was stenciled on the cinder block:
Remember your level.
The toneless bell sounded.
Doors opened, nobody inside.
Then, who knows why, a rod of light
at the base of my skull flashed
to every outpost of my far-flung body—
I've got my life back.
It was nothing, just the present moment
occurring for the first time in months.
My head translated light,
my eyes spiked with tears.
The awful green walls, I could have stroked them.
The dirt, the moving cube I stepped into—
it was all beautiful,
everything that took me up.

Who We Will Love

FOR PHEBE HANSON

The old man from the next cabin is inspecting the rocks.
He has a jeweler's eyepiece, and the picnic table is covered
with Pre-Cambrian chunks of Lake Superior.
This shoreline looks like the Maine coast,
the oceanic breakers, the boulders jutting out
to meet the water like the north Atlantic shelf.
This old man is our best example of New England.
He is tall, the lean puritan body bends with stern attention
over the marvelous multiplicity of God's plainness,
the repetitive rocks, the limitless plate of unbroken water,
the unbudging glacial history of the boulders
that speaks of the slowness of violent change.
He has attended to all of this for forty summers.
He is so beautiful, we all want to fall in love
with stoical ministers who are charred with doubt,
with watchmakers who repair fine old timepieces,
with farmers who wake up early to split oak logs
and stack them in piles for winter.
We'll fall in love with anyone who
takes his time, who looks, who agrees
to keep looking for forty years at least,
who believes in the truth of the microscope,
whose head gets whiter and frailer every summer,
whose response to the wind-blown opening
of the wild rose is, "Yes, correct."
He must believe in the rigorous clock of the seasons,
he must be able to count.
Beyond that, his time is his own.
The spiderwebs hoisted between the starry asters
that shiver with cold dew,
the sleek timothy grass and the hair of the buffalo grass,
the raspberry bushes, the gooseberries
in their thorny lives, the silky black-and-white skunk
who turned shyly, who did not want to fight,

142

the young seagull whose feathers are still mottled
like the egg he came from,
the stones, the stones, the stones,
the lapping fresh water, the soft, unfired
bowl that holds the water:
we will love
who loves all this.

LINDA BACK McKAY (B. 1947)

Watermelon Hill

"CLOSE THE DOOR AND NEVER LOOK BACK.
THIS IS FINISHED FOR YOU NOW."
—SISTER MARIE DOLORES

After she got herself in trouble, they sent her
away to Watermelon Hill, which was not really
its name, but what the boys yelled to the swollen girls
who were to come due at that home for unwed mothers.
A crucifix glared from the roof.
Laurel Taylor was not her real name.
What was real was absolved by Mother
Superior with a flap of her cloak.
Under the Immaculate Heart of Mary
was posted a litany of daily chores.
Miles of buffed linoleum, bars on the windows,
Doctor Crutchfield on Wednesdays, jelly jars
filled with vitamins. The tables were set for forty
or so, depending on who was in labor.
The tuna casseroles smelled like bleach.
Girls back from the hospital sat on donut pillows.
Days passed and the moon sickened.

Laurel Taylor, on her horrible cot with the stars
burning inside her, tried to pray.
It was best to give up your baby, not see or hold it.
It was best to place your baby, make a plan for it.

Laurel Taylor tried to pray in chapel,
her cardigan sweater open like a gate.
She fought to be good, to give her blood to some
nice family, to cleanse a child from her name.
Laurel Taylor tried to keep the monsters away
but under some god's baleful eye, they rose
in a spine-cramping pain that was only the start
of the tearing off.

She lost her son in that war. Wading in water,
being able to see her feet again, she knew there would be
no anointing, no Extreme Unction.
After signing the surrender, she knew
the penance is fault and the loss is eternal.

Nancy Frederiksen (b. 1948)

Flying Blue Angel

You were leader of the pack
and it had been brave of me
to trust in you,
meet you at the rink
lace our skates
in the warming house
tune our rhythm to the
Flying Blue Angels crackling
from a make-shift loudspeaker
hooked to the top of an old car.

Freshman year, Mother said
"Tell that boy good-bye"
and I handed out her verdict.
You took it as if it belonged
to you, fit like a second skin.

Years later, the woman you
married left
with bruises traced back to you,
further back then to your father.
Did the hand that held mine, do that?

My heart disbelieves
remembers
only the music
daredevils of the sky
arms linked in trust

hearts wide open.

Jean Jacobson (b. 1948)

Skater

Not a sound but the creak of ice,
the screeking of white leather;
Not a sound but a huffing of breath;
skater alone here, age twelve, silent
arms symmetrical as branches and hands
counterweights adjusting her balance,
higher, or lower, riding the glide
of the body; not a notion but the narrow
feel of the stiff boots and the quickness
of steel skating the rough ice with
a guttering sound, she begins a long curve,
on one foot, on the outside edge,
free leg a pendulum swung at the turn:
This is The Figure Eight. Finished,
she looks back, fists tucking the waist,
begins again

> the continuous figure.
> Picture a woman of middle age,
> drowsy among the squeaks of age
> and the sharper precision of memory;
> picture the pen nib skating a page,
> the sound of scratches and looping.
> A cold draft from the past steadies
> the skater, sets a blade deeper
> into the ice, on the inside edge; the pen
> draws its figure: Little skater
> dipped in ink, curving back along this
> long figure, passing smoothly, pressing
> her likeness into the icy page, look in,
> look out, knowing what it is
> to be alone with the feel
> of that steel neatly cutting
> the fresh surface.

Patricia Kirkpatrick (b. 1949)

A Road in Northern Minnesota

passes men mowing shoulders of clover
summer afternoons,
the drums of the highway crew
pouring tar over surfaces
mute as the box turtle, yellow as toadflax.
I don't say you'll be safe on this road
where blackbirds and sparrows
stash business in ditches
and the come-upon goldfinches
rise when they're startled.
If I glance ahead to standing water
I might see a moose or something larger.
Probably not in Crow Wing County.
But that's why I love this road—it lets me see
what isn't here.
One night when we came back from town
the road lifted its hill
to touch the earth's invisible charges.
Aurora borealis,
light stroking the dome overhead.
We stopped the car and got out in the road
to exchange names with the stars.
Tell the stars who you are, we told the children.
Tell the bear and the arrow and the sisters of fire
where you want the road to take you.

Joyce Sutphen (b. 1949)

What to Pack

Either nothing you've ever worn before
or everything old and warm. Only
one of anything, but bring along all

of something. Don't forget a few worthless
items so you can leave what you really
need at home. Pack lightly and pack often;

practice packing in the middle of night.
Before you fall asleep, picture the trip
you have always wanted to take and pack

the things you'll need there· a lute, a pear tree,
and a dove the color of a cloud packed
with thousands of raindrops, each one of them

standing at the open door in the sky
with a ticket and a tiny suitcase.

Vicki Graham (b. 1950)

Solstice

Glacial ridge: dry grass
burns bronze at sunset

and the oaks hold their leaves late
into winter.   She matches

her fingers to their lobes,
then learns to want snow

the way her heart wants silence.
Wind rattles sumac

at the thicket's edge, breaks
milkweed pods.   Seed

falls like snow on snowless
earth and the voles cringe

in their burrows. She follows
the sun's slow arc west

as though she were the shadow
of a branch, leaving no prints

on wind-burnt turf as birds
leave no prints in air.   Memory,

like fear, reinscribes itself,
but here, cold completes

desire, molds her heart
to the moment. Wanting snow

is one way of wanting nothing:
the silence at dusk

when the wind drops
and the owl swoops from the oaks.

Margaret Hasse (b. 1950)

In a Sheep's Eye, Darling

To Yofe, to Richard, to marriage

All day in biology class you'd been looking hard
at everything put in front of you on the counter
as if you were starving for these sights:
a tree frog's beating heart, lichen from a tree,
swamp water's industrious community.
Even wax from your ear under a magnifying glass
made you bend lower, awed at the gunk
your body produces.
If this is what we slough off, how amazing
attached cells must be, you thought, and carefully
scraped some from the inside of your cheek.
The cells were blurred, like a smudged charcoal
drawing, just the way you imagined cheek cells
to be, not the precision of liver, not brain.
You knew you didn't know much about this,
and were probably wrong, but you loved
your own excitement, as if you were the first
person to open another in an operation
and discover all the organs under
a slipcover of fascia like tender offspring.

All this looking set you up to be stunned by the eye.
And you stared back at the big dismembered thing,
the way it sat in its socket like a pearl
in a soft oyster, like an oiled, see-through marble.
The cornea, tiny and perfect in its convexity,
and the lens, the way it flattened and thickened
in the center, white irregular filaments running
through it, as if some sight shattered inside
or some sight held, all sewn up.

The teacher thought it unlikely your wife
would share your thrill, but let you
carry the eye home in your backpack,
in the baggie left over from lunch, and you two
bent over it in the bright fluorescence of kitchen
and noticed the irrigation system of blood vessels
and the soggy iris, and the cornea
and talked about what you could see being
only the tiniest part of the eye, and the eye
only a small part of the sheep, and the sheep
a small part of the farm and the earth and the universe
and you went to bed too awed to have sex.
That night you dreamed of the great grass
of sheep fields, the way it looked to the sheep
who stuck her head into it seeking
a particular blade, and the color green
welled up inside you like tears, and you woke.

Deborah Keenan (b. 1950)

Loving Motels

Feels American.
Shameless, somehow.
People I don't know
Love motels. People
I don't know love chlorine;
Hundreds and thousands of people
I know and don't know
Love motel pools, whirlpools,
Hot tubs, saunas.
People I love, people who love
Me, those people love room service.
The sheer
Intellectual weight: the idea of a phone,
Wires, another phone, then food arriving.
Preposterous and sexual.
Sexy, like those bathing suits
You only wear in pools
In motels in Montreal, or
Pools in Shawnee Mission, any pool
Where no one you know will walk by
And know you.
Loving motels means loving
What has not rooted in your spirit.
Loving motels is loving
Your very own ice bucket,
And the special shapes the ice takes,
Is loving the shining cans of pop
Sinking through the melting ice,
The sound aluminum makes
While you pretend to sleep,
Is loving the hidden air conditioners
And the cable TV shows, and is
Letting no one else, not even someone
You love, use your own wrapped

Bar of soap, or your own little pack
Of ten-month-old Sanka
Or the sweet little hotplate
That just fits the baby coffee pot.
People like me and including me
Love motels for the white towels
Which remind us of something large
We have lost somewhere. We love
The deep shag carpet we would hate
At home. We love the key,
The number, the simple locks,
Not like home where locks are hard,
Needing a hip thrown against
The door, the dead bolt really dead,
We love the simple key with the simple
Plastic shape: sometimes a fish,
Sometimes a smooth, beige oval,
Sometimes, if we are lucky,
A shamrock, a clover, a doll, or dog.
We love motels for letting us
Drive up, we get our own parking space
Automatically, then we get love-
Making that is not connected
To our own bed's history,
And besides the white towels
We get white sheets
Which we all love and never buy.
We get left alone,
We get the feeling of being alone,
And we need America to leave us
Alone in the motels.

Ethna McKiernan (b. 1951)

The Scholar in the Playroom

My father's head was propped up in his hands.
Around him chaos swirled; the cello played
off-key in practice, someone vacuumed sand
we'd tracked in from the beach. I was amazed

that he could concentrate through all of this,
scoring Shakespeare's words with yellow pen
and calmly reading as I wrestled Fergus
while the youngest blundered through the den.

For years I've carried my father's image around,
the flame in the storm who loved the crazy wind
his children were despite the din of sound
he sometimes wished he could rescind.

He proved the ivory tower a myth, this anti-Lear,
who kept his children, his Cordelias near.

CarolAnn Russell (b. 1951)

Fishing

The warmest waters beckon
and blind. Once I believed
time could be owned, returned to,
that I could find my childhood
the way I find a grave.

A man fishes all day beneath the sun.
He could be my father leaving
the river, body like a tree,
the root invisible, come to rest
in the sparse farmyard remembered
as it was before the burial.
No name to touch him, his face
becomes a star
and three white horses follow.

I consider the peril of any relation, hooks
caught in the lip of the eyeless
trout, living off its entrails.

In the tea-colored afternoon,
a man walks toward dusk.
He carries a basket, three
silver fish, their open mouths
pools of milk in the dark.
It might be August
or Christmas, the toothed faces
of the aster, blooming,
the tide of the man
flooding an acre of tamarack.
He sees only the light leaving
the valley. In the absence,
his soul like a bell.

Fishing demands belief:
the line cast out
reeled back again.

Ann Taylor Sargent (b. 1951)

21 Postcards

I flip through the book: my home town
seen through the lens of a landscape photographer.
Seen superbly—no airbrushed color
as in dimestore postcards,
no Greetings from the Land of Old Cars.
They make me want to live here,
yet they let me know I don't,
not in this city without billboards
or dandelions or phone poles.
I'm drawn to it and yet disturbed,
so I proofread it against the city I know.
Here's Hennepin Avenue,
the building I see from my bus stop:
red brick with a purple staircase.
But you can't tell they sell music there,
you can't see what's playing at the Skyway next door.
Everything at street level's been cropped out;
everything commercial or pedestrian.
The beautiful city starts one flight up,
its nose in the air with the clouds
and the skyscrapers. I page to a church in St. Paul—
no denomination's posted, no parishioners appear.
No lobbyists clutter this hall in the Capitol.
No cars can be seen on this downtown bridge,
their passing diluted to invisibility.
I wish I could minimize cars by long exposure.
My city is framed by a windshield,
the city of stoplights and parking lots,
grocery stores and gas stations. My city
has a daughter in the middle of a softball field.
There's a lawn that needs mowing
and a counter for sorting mail,
for turning over postcards that have stubbed corners,
postcards that have somehow lived.

My city has a television in the living room,
a computer dead center on the desk,
a book off to one side. Close-ups of familiar faces,
backgrounds out of focus. My city is fast food restaurants,
the Black Forest patio I wait all winter to dine on,
shopping malls and the sale table outside Borders Books
where I stand now, thumbing through this book
of postcards, entranced by the saturated color,
by the light streaming behind the boat
that was faster than film.
My city is not this gorgeous ghost town,
awash in the colors of dusk and dawn.
But I love seeing it so beautifully distorted.
I buy two copies: one to keep, one to send.
Wish I was here.

Marisha Chamberlain (b. 1952)

Winter Washday

You collected snow every day of the week
and melted it in a barrel inside the door.
Through with the dark things, two days
on the washboard in that strong, lye water,
your fingers would all gather.
Sheets and the white things boiled on the stove
with soap shaved off with a sharp knife,
and you fished them out on a long stick,
holding them out from you, scalding hot,
sliding them into the rinse water.
They hung outside 'til they froze dry,
the long johns and overalls,
standing up stiff and laughable,
and you brought them inside and stood them
against the wall, the whole house
growing cold because of them,
until, all at once, they would clump down wet
like somebody falling out of bed,
and you strung them on the line that crossed the room.
In the dark, you stumbled between lines
of clothes, every night of the winter,
dreaming that you had to launder the snow,
gathering sheets of it into your tub
while more fell through the bleaching air
and your husband pushed you away in his sleep
from the handfuls of cloth you were scrubbing
over the ridge of his backbone.

MARY LOGUE (B. 1952)

Song in Killeshandra

Toward the end they ask Seamus to sing.
An old man lifts a wee girl
to his knee and gives her a taste of
foamy Guinness. The rain teems
through the night. We are safe.

Seamus lifts the shoulders of his shirt,
runs a finger down his thin nose and then,
like a wren, throws his head back and begins
to sing the song that we all know,
the words little changed, of loss and love

and loss and luck and we hope so much and get
so little. Something settles on us as we
breathe in the smoke-plumed air.
His voice flies in circles
and we watch as the bird batters his wings.

If only a window would open, the sky
would break, releasing his voice of trills
and valleys. Seamus sings the song
that our mothers taught us and our fathers
hummed coming home in the dark.

Francine Sterle (b. 1952)

Flat-backed Fox

Who lives on the forest border.
Who crawls from a cave beneath the roots of a stump, crawls
from the sandy apron of soil spilling from his den.

Who buts at beetles and butterflies until one day,
launching into an arcing leap,
lands forepaws first on a startled vole.

Who can be coaxed out of hiding
by kissing the back of your hand,
mimicking the sounds of a squealing rodent,

but who vanishes amid dense scrub-growth,
blends to his surroundings, moving
the way the wind moves through a field of wheat.

Whose soft yap chases meadow mice into the leaves.
Whose tracks form a perfectly dotted line.
Whose tracks follow the railroad's punctuated ties.

Who is deliberate in his movements.
Who does not know the agility of his track.
Who does not complicate the world with these abstractions.

Whose steady eye stalks song birds and ground squirrels.
Who does not apologize for his cunning.
Whose every sense wakens in the chirping air.

Fox whose tail is russet red.
Whose tail is a brush fire.
Whose burning tail flashes in flight.

Connie Wanek (b. 1952)

Jump Rope

There is menace
in its relentless course, round and round,
describing an ellipsoid,
an airy prison in which a young girl
is incarcerated.

Whom will she marry? Whom will she love?
The rope, like a snake,
has the gift of divination,
yet reveals only a hint, a single initial.
But what if she never misses?

Is competence its own reward?
Will the rope never strike her ankle,
love's bite? The enders turn and turn,
two-handed as their arms tire,
their enchantments exhausted.

It hurts to watch her now,
flushed and scowling,
her will stronger than her limbs,
her braids lashing her shoulders
with each small success.

Louise Erdrich (b. 1954)

Advice to Myself

Leave the dishes.
Let the celery rot in the bottom drawer of the refrigerator
and an earthen scum harden on the kitchen floor.
Leave the black crumbs in the bottom of the toaster.
Throw the cracked bowl out and don't patch the cup.
Don't patch anything. Don't mend. Buy safety pins.
Don't even sew on a button.
Let the wind have its way, then the earth
that invades as dust and then the dead
foaming up in gray rolls underneath the couch.
Talk to them. Tell them they are welcome.
Don't keep all the pieces of the puzzles
or the doll's tiny shoes in pairs, don't worry
who uses whose toothbrush or if anything
matches, at all.
Except one word to another. Or a thought.
Pursue the authentic—decide first
what is authentic,
then go after it with all your heart.
Your heart, that place
you don't even think of cleaning out.
That closet stuffed with savage mementos.
Don't sort the paper clips from screws from saved baby teeth
or worry if we're all eating cereal for dinner
again. Don't answer the telephone, ever,
or weep over anything at all that breaks.
Pink molds will grow within those sealed cartons
in the refrigerator. Accept new forms of life
and talk to the dead
who drift in through the screened windows, who collect
patiently on the tops of food jars and books.
Recycle the mail, don't read it, don't read anything
except what destroys
the insulation between yourself and your experience
or what pulls down or what strikes at or what shatters
this ruse you call necessity.

Owls

The barred owls scream in the black pines,
searching for mates. Each night
the noise wakes me, a death
rattle, everything in sex that wounds.
There is nothing in the sound but raw need
of one feathered body for another.
Yet, even when they find each other,
there is no peace.

In Ojibwe, the owl is Kokoko, and not
even the smallest child loves the gentle sound
of the word. Because the hairball
of bones and vole teeth can be hidden
under snow, to kill the man who walks over it.
Because the owl looks behind itself to see you coming,
the vane of the feather does not disturb
air, and the barb is ominously soft.

Have you ever seen, at dusk,
an owl take flight from the throat of a dead tree?
Mist, troubled spirit.
You will notice only after
its great silver body has turned to bark.
The flight was soundless.
That is how we make love,
when there are people in the halls around us,
clashing dishes, filling their mouths
with air, with debris, pulling
switches and filters as the whole machinery
of life goes on, eliminating and eliminating
until there were just the two bodies
fiercely attached, the feathers
floating down and cleaving to their shapes.

Rez Litany

Let us now pray to those beatified
within the Holy Colonial church
beginning with Saint Assimilus,
patron of residential and of government
boarding schools, whose skin was dark
but who miraculously bled white milk
for all to drink.
To cure the gut aches that resulted
as ninety percent of Native children are
lactose intolerant, let us now pray to the
patron saint of the Indian Health Service,
who is also guardian of slot machines,
Our Lady of Luck, she who carries
in one hand mistaken blood tests and botched
surgeries and in the other hand the heart
of a courageous doctor squeezed dry.
Let us pray for the sacred hearts of all good doctors
and nurses, whose tasks are manifold and made more difficult
by the twin saints of commodity food,
Saint Bloatinus and Saint Cholestrus,
who were martyred at the stake of body fat
and who preside now in heaven
at the gates of the Grand Casino Buffet.
Saint Macaronia and Saint Diabeta, hear our prayer.
It is terrible to be diminished toe by toe.
Good Saint Pyromane,
Enemy of the BIA,
Deliver us from those who seek to bury us
in files and triplicate documents and directives.
Saint Quantum, Martyr of Blood
and Holy Protector of the Tribal Rolls,
assist us in the final shredding which shall proceed
on the Day of Judgment so we may all rain down
in a blizzard of bum pull tabs
and unchosen lottery tickets, which represent
the souls of the faithfully departed
in your name.

Your name written in the original fire
we mistook so long ago for trader's rum.
Pray for us, all you saints of white port
four roses old granddad and night train.
Good Saint Bingeous who fell asleep upside down on the cross
and rose on the third day without even knowing he had died.
Saint Odium of the hundred-proof blood
and Saint Tremens of the great pagan spiders
dripping from the light fixtures.
You powerful triumvirate, intercede for us
drunks stalled in the bars,
float our asses off the cracked stools
and over to the tribal college,
where the true saints are ready to sacrifice their brain cells
for our brain cells, in that holy exchange which is called learning.
Saint Microcephalia, patron of huffers and dusters,
you of the cooked brain and mean capacity, you
of the simian palm line and poor impulse control,
you of the Lysol-soaked bread, you sleeping with the dogs
underneath the house, hear our prayers
which we utter backwards and sideways
as nothing makes sense
least of all your Abstinence Campaign
from which Oh Lord Deliver Us.
Saints Primapara, Gravida, and Humpenenabackseat,
you patrons of unsafe teenage sex
and fourteen-year-old mothers,
pray for us now and at the hour of our birth,
amen.

Gail Rixen (b. 1954)

Shell River

Shell River came down to us smelling just enough
of fish and something exotic, wound around
our sandy oxbows and left a few to grow over.
There were people upstream and downstream
and we wanted to row and we didn't.

The flood and lean of seasons gave and denied
and then bit and swallowed the south bank
foot by foot. All along the undecided edge
thin browned children came here and there
to wait for something to wash down.

Just gaping clamshells and broken spirals
of lakeweed tumbled all the way to us.
Beer cans from the land of sky-blue waters,
all empty, and we forgot waiting.

In the flooded shallows, bugs lived in their own
twig bundles and many-legged aliens scooted
between last-year's grass blades and northerns
wove through the channels cows' hooves made
in the hungry summers till when a car growled by
we didn't look up anymore.

Susan Steger Welsh (b. 1954)

In Defense of Semicolons

As a child I had no use for them,
preferring instead the firm
grip of conjunctions, the certainty
of the full stop, the way
commas can stall
a bedtime.
A master poet says
don't use them; they're ugly.
You have to admire a man
who'll take a stand
on punctuation.
        But how else
can you keep the family together?
Some things want to move
slowly; a dash would be wrong.
Not the smear of rain on a windshield,
but a snowflake in the palm
of a parent's glove.
        The world is full
of lists, and commas give way
under pressure. The homely semicolon
holds, a full moon floating
above the ocean's chop,
the undertow of history, waves
of events separated
by breath—my breath, your breath,
it doesn't matter.
        As a child,
I would have given everything
for beauty, but I'm past that.
Now I can see how much hinges
on punctuation, the small
clear marks we use to find our place.

Sandy Beach (b. 1955)

Slow Brown Fox

This fox fur collar, given to me by my grandmother
the only animal in my home, no longer holds
the odor of Pall Malls, guilt, and Gordon's Gin.

Well over 70 years old·
it is sensual,
it is beautiful,
it is dead.

I can't bring myself to wear it or get rid of it.

Sometimes, I wrap it
into a chair as if it were sleeping
its little paws peeping
out from beneath its tail.

CANDACE BLACK (B. 1955)

Vigil

The seasonal croup had filled the ward
with children struggling for air,
telltale barks in foggy tents. I lived

in the reclining chair
next to Keenan's caged crib, slipping
my hand beneath the plastic

to hold his into sleep, the electronic
blip of a baby's heart
monitor our erratic lullabye.

When the nurses floated in at 4
they *were* angels: silently
efficient as they charted fever and liquid

intake, changed soggy
sheets while I held the mask of therapeutic
vapor to my son's face and crooned

him calm. I believed in his daily
improvement, but I could not leave him.
My breath was tied to his, each fit

of coughing jolting me
awake. I stayed three days underwater,
surfacing on our way home

to find it irreversibly autumn, leaves
fallen and crackling underfoot.

Kate Lynn Hibbard (b. 1956)

Kleptomania

Aunt Alma was a kleptomaniac,
and summers she would show up at our farm
with Uncle Ben and hints of Aberdeen,
a trail of peignoir sets and macaroons,
her stealing not accounted for by need.
A glamorous disease, or so it seemed,
to take instead of learning not to want,
that working class cliché she never bought.
She'd thirst for more of everything instead,
spring onions, sex with men she didn't love.
The marriage doctor diagnosed abuse,
an absent father, something more profound.
That wasn't half the story. Why should she
be called a common thief for seeking heat?

Leslie Adrienne Miller (b. 1956)

Up North

I've had too much champagne, a sip
of cognac, a few blue hits on the good cigar
handed round at midnight in the blast
of bonfire on the frozen lake,

so we hurry back into our woods, drive
as far as the road is cleared, then toss
the bright plastic sled on the snow
where I lay me down to ride the last

half mile in. Prone, I see no more
than branches clasped above; cold pulls
its stilling finger along my spine,
and I hold my blood against it

to see what will push back. The snow
is deep but light, gives with shush
as I slip through, erase my lover's tracks.
He stops on hills, shifts his weight,

changes hands on the burning rope.
He's pulled in everything on sleds before,
wood, water, gear, boxes of wine and meat,
but never a woman, a weight that warms

the track and leaves a long gash of ice.
I brace my heels against the sled's hard rim,
The snow's chaff riding in around my thighs.
I know he wants this dark work of hauling me

to see if he can bear my weight, to dream me
as a stone, a corpse, pure sure thing.
And me, I'm not opposed to playing chattel
or spoil, allowing how he has to pull away

and lean against the dark to haul me up
hard against his heels. I let him have
the pleasure of dragging home his woman,
offer up my inert flesh as ballast, balance

against desire's dogged march into the dark.

Bridal Wear

The aisles of frocks whitecap on their racks,
and I want someone to go in for me, find
the one without beads, sequins, blisters of lace.
I can't abide the leagues of white, thickets of silk

and tulle, sateen gloves, baskets wrapped in net and puff.
I swoon with headache from the sickened store air,
the gowns gassed in truckloads before they left
Malaysia or Taiwan. Imposter in the bridal *shoppe*,

I'm middle-aged, doubtful, even appalled by the project,
but here nonetheless, looking, like everyone else,
for the perfect fog of organdy or taffeta in which
to meet the lover I want to be my last. I drop

the bargain dress over my head in a hall of mirrors
that rivals Versailles, step up on the block
and float my image in champagne satin,
ashamed I've even found one dress to want.

The price tags flutter and beckon. The beadwork
loosens and ticks as I twirl. But everyone around me
donning gowns grows more beautiful, impossible
to miss: giant bleached insects with their cinched waists

and bubbled breasts, wads of train fizzing behind them.
Outside it's a September afternoon, one of the last
warm days, slow bees beading the muggy air,
an afternoon when I ought to be in a canoe

with my lover, sequins of river light spreading out
behind us, a bottle of wine in the dry sack,
my oar dipped in the slowed autumn current
of the Cannon, and behind me, my intended

dipping with me, so we move together as if
down an aisle, though with the peace
of perfect assurance that where we're headed
matters much less than where we are.

SHEILA PACKA (B. 1956)

The Vermilion Trail

I am leaving
the Mesabi Iron Range
on the same trail
that a gold prospector
came in on,
with a compass gone
awry and red dust
on my boots.
Me, the daughter
of a cat skinner
born on the Divide.
I can say we got by.
In my pocket is the copper
penny of my childhood,
once I reforged it
on the DM&IR
track south of Biwabik.
My father hung a lead pipe
between two pines
in the yard, the somersault
around the pole was
"skin the cat."
I was good.
I never crossed
a picket line,
never scabbed.
Worship was in
the union hall.
If we got a raise
that was why.
Payday was playing
a jukebox in the bar,
dancing with a pool stick.

Whisky was a life
waiting for somebody
to marry it.
I laid myself off,
packed my trunk,
picked up where my immigrant
past left off.
I'll write when I find work.

WANG PING (B. 1957)

Opening The Face

She comes in,
thread between her teeth,
the "lady of wholesome fortune,"
two sons, three daughters,
husband in government service,
parents-in-law healthy and content,
surrounded by laughing grandchildren.
Mother paid her gold to open
my face on my wedding day.

"Sit still," she orders, twining
the cotton thread to test its strength.
"It hurts, but nothing like footbinding,
or the hardship of a newlywed."
She pulls it through her teeth,
lines it against my forehead.
Wet, cold, it furrows into the skin,
into the roots of my virgin down.
The uprooted hair hisses
after the twanging thread.

"Don't make a sound, girl," she whispers
to my drenched face, "not until you bear him a son,
not until you have grandchildren."
She holds her breath as she scrapes
between the eyebrows and lashes, opens
her mouth again when she reaches for the cheek.
"What's ten, twenty, or even thirty years?
We came to this world with nothing but
patience. You have high cheekbones
and a big nose, signs of a man-killer,
but compensated by a round chin.
Just keep your mouth shut, eyes open.
There, there," she leans closer, wiping
beads of tears from my eyelashes.

I turn to the light, my face
a burning field.

"Now you're ready for the big day."
Her fingers trace along my cheekbones.
"Your face clean and open.
I'll cover it with a red scarf.
The only person who can lift
the veil is your groom. All other eyes
are evil eyes. Remember, remember."

She puts on her shoes.
"Ah, one more thing," she leans to my ear,
her breath steaming with pickled mustard greens,
yellow rice wine, its bitter sweetness
from years of fermentation in a sealed jar
deep underground. Her secret
tickles the inside of my ear.
"When he sleeps, put your shoes
in his boots and let them sit overnight.
It'll keep him under your thumb, forever."

What Holds

when eyes cradle a lover's curve
when a bee hums in the throat of a rose

when baby girls cry out on streets, nameless
young mothers hovering in nearby woods

when birds feast on cicada nymphs
ending a seventeen-year dream in the deep

when a four-year-old shouts
my heart's on fire

trees, bugs, fish
an ocean begins in a drop of rain

at dawn
a broad-leaf epiphyllum blossoms

we live, fear notwithstanding
memory holds us to this world

JANE WHITLEDGE (B. 1957)

What It Was Like

It was a wide blue lake
unless it was a pond.
The shore was mostly sand
golden in the sun,
unless the shore was rock cliff,
no place to rest. I pushed on
against head winds, whitecaps,
unless I glided on a surface
still as ease, a glass dream.
Now and then there was
an island with clearing enough
for bed and campfire, unless
the island was a tangle of deadfall,
dry fir harsh as barbed-wire,
jumbled rock underfoot,
yellow-jackets in the thickets.
Or I pressed on and slept
in my canoe, a fine cocoon,
a floating willow leaf or,
in the dark, a bassinet rocking
me gently under stars, unless
it was a coffin, unless
the mosquitoes buzzed and thrived
on my misery of toss and turn.
The weather was always idyllic,
picture-book blue, unless dark
wet, no sun for a week.
And there were always blueberries,
sweet and plentiful
on rock-and-pine island slopes
above glinting water, below
billowy summer clouds,
unless there were brown-
bitten leaves on drought-brittle hills,

and bones of wolf-kill
unless there was a fawn
springing to its feet.
There was always wildlife
unless there was only shadow
and boulder alive in the brush.
And the fish were always biting
unless they were not.
There was always belief
unless there was doubt.
And the waves were always
coming in, unless they were
going out.

Ellie Schoenfeld (b. 1958)

If I Were the Moon

If I were the moon
I would turn your tide.
You would draw maps of me,
would want to learn everything
about my topography,
you would lick me to see
if I am made of green cheese or not.
You would memorize the names
of my mountains and seas.
If I were the moon
you would watch for me,
you would study my face and my curves
and the way my movements
make shadow pictures on your walls.
If I were the moon
you would smile at me
and I would climb in through your window.
I would fill your room
with my own particular madness inducing
lunacy producing light.
I would shine on you and make you howl
until I could taste my name
on your lips and in your mouth.

Diane Jarvenpa (b. 1959)

Night Walk to the Sauna

This is all chicory and cold shale,
wormwood and shinleaf
where my mother holds high the lantern
to step around the wasp nest
and stinging nettles,
through the humid night
prickly as thimbleberries,
along this path where crows kick rain off leaves
and the bats staccato-dive insect clouds.
We move slowly for the old pines
send out tentacle roots
and the low catch of spider webs
stitch sudden death blooms.
We follow the lake scent of iron and fish scale
to the sweet dry smoke of birch
where my mother feeds the stove
in the small wooden room,
where I come out of the long darkness,
eyes filmy, hair sea of green, feet of thorns
and shed my little-girl meanness,
that tight slick slide of shell
to a wash of gold and pink,
lungs of steam,
awkward limbs filled with new slim muscle
and my mother all fireweed and wood lily.
Our two pumping hearts
like one blood moon rising higher,
our warm bones, hissing stars
running through the wild mint
and that acre of lake that licks us clean.

ATHENA KILDEGAARD (B. 1959)

After the Death of His Brother's Wife

Uncle Jack, the oldest, says
From now on it's a lottery.
He means Don't count on me
to die next. I may be the oldest,
I may have lied before any of you,
gotten drunk first, fucked a girl first,
but this time, boys, don't count on me.

Maybe they would whisper,
Jack, show us the way,
as if the way were visible,
something other
than the brightest darkness,
an unfolding of a flat thing,
a certainty weighed against itself.

What he means is, I'm afraid—
and if they could, his brothers
would say to him Yes, yes—

Kathryn Kysar (b. 1960)

The Pregnant Wife Eats Dirt

It is gray everywhere: coal soot
on the eaves, rain changes to sleet
changes to dirty white snow. We
have nothing to eat but potatoes,
turnips, and bread. I crave
green: braised kale, spinach,
even shredded cabbage.
The sky is pregnant too—full
of scudding round clouds.
I barter the ring for a cabbage,
make soup, but it doesn't satisfy.

One night, when they are all asleep,
I touch the tip of my tongue to a sliver of coal,
but it is gritty, dusty, and black.
The next day, the children napping,
I take a tablespoon into the garden
dig under the icy layer of snow to the gray clay dirt
beside the fence. I put the spoon to my mouth.
It tastes of aluminum, feces, and clay pots.
I dip my spoon in again, lift it to my lips,
then hear my neighbor splashing her wash water
out the door. I stand, smooth my apron,
slipping the spoon inside the pocket,
wanting the sky to darken, the moon
to open up and swallow me, feed me
rocks and gold, minerals and diamonds,
all the hardness in the world
to make this soft baby grow.

ELIZABETH ONESS (B. 1960)

Belleek

> I AM TROUBLED, I'M DISSATISFIED, I'M IRISH.
> -MARIANNE MOORE

For years I resisted it, the only
shatterable part of my inheritance—

china sprinkled with insipid shamrocks,
two tones of green, the sweetly clustered leaves

bordering the plates in an Irish ring-a-rosy,
unfurling from the teapot's stalk

like a fairy invention, a porcelain version of
a time that never was.

There was no blarney in the house where I grew up.
We were tight-lipped, silent;
                              superfluity was sin.

Nothing to do? I'll give you something to do.
You want something to cry about? I'll give you something...

My grandmother cried leaving Ireland the last time.
I sat beside her on the plane

staring down at the Cliffs of Moher,
water breaking over the wrack-mired stone.

She had shown me the house where she grew up,
the nettled fields, the barn

where her father locked her in a stall
and she stayed all night afraid
                                and no one let her out.

A vine of angry fathers, mothers porcelain pale.

When I left my father's house
I too knew it would be my final visit.

But I left without tears, shook the dust from my feet,
the only nostalgia a wordless music.

I was as guilty as anyone. I knew it.

Every time I opened my mouth there was drama,
accusation, but my words fell on whiskey

dissolved in that distillate warmth.

And still this problem with the china—
unadorned it would be lovely,

translucent weave of white on white,
the palest gloss of yellow

tipped inside the teapot's stem.
It's the sentiment that spoils it,

as if the unembellished can't be pleasing.
I want a teapot bearing

each denial of the body, bitterness and bad teeth.

But even the blemished past isn't
                        unembellished truth.

The darker truth
is what's confided. Her whisper

whispers through me now: *Come here little one....*
Come here 'till I tell you.

Kirsten Dierking (b. 1962)

Northern Oracle

The aluminum prow scratches over
submerged vines, drifts through platters
of lily-pads. I lean to the side,
rest my hand on the water, touch
the sky of unknowable swimmers
feeding beneath me.

Sometimes I think the future begins
at the bottom of lakes. The next day rising
toward sound and action and easier
breathing. Darkness wanting
the candor of daylight, the simple shapes
of high noon, the plain faces with no
shadows.

I watch for an omen, but three feet
down, the sun disappears into murk
and secrets. The waves are reading
the lines of my palm, but show only this:
tomorrow coming like shimmering scales,
like transient bones fanned into dazzling,
silver fins.

Betsy Brown (b. 1963)

Hallways of a Diamond: January 2004

Little Henry
is six now.
He collects maps.
His journeys secret,
run at bent speed,
cow-licked and revved,
all his sidewalk
chase scenes located.
Coordinate. Keyed.
His cities ordered.
His parks defined,
corridors fit
to locate rightly,
classroom, kitchen,
hotel room with foldout,
the arrow, steel
handrail descending
purple stairwells
adult-led, lit.
He draws towers
and fires, watches
for torrents, free
falls of moonlight
chainlinked over frost,
brilliant-cut facets
the blueprints of boyhood,
the pause and haunts
of dares that were
someone else's
to lose—the spilled,
the last second,

a vanished window,
frozen ladder
twisting now suncaught,
dangling from its crane
above this lost ground,
the shot-for, imprinted,
scaffolded and constant,
to light, to guard,
to steady now, to find.

HEID ERDRICH (B. 1963)

Animoosh

A girl surrounded by brothers
has to have a dream. Mine
was to live deep in green woods
near a stream with a dog to protect me.
Not the family dog, that pile of lint
who licked and begged, but some dream
dog who would mysteriously appear.
Heroic canine—swift as a Greyhound,
she'd share her kill. Her markings
would be expressive as a Shepherd's,
mobile brows and a smiling muzzle.
She'd be velvet-pelted as a Bulldog
and as big-jawed to pull me from sink holes,
mud slides. I'd call the mutt Annie,
and when we rested on the cold earth,
breathing the same raw-rabbit breath,
far from home, darkness creaking about us,
Annie's ears twitching, tail swishing—
we could howl all our loneliness into the world.

I was sure that dog would come from my dream.
With my back to the shadow edge of the shelter belt,
I would stare until I saw her—always just beyond me,
bounding through the long field of goldenrod and sun.

Animoosh IS OJIBWAY FOR *dog*.

Stung

She couldn't help but sting my fingers,
clinging a moment before I flung her
to the ground. Her gold is true, not the trick
evening light plays on my roses.
She curls into herself, stinger twitching
gilt wings folded. Her whole life just a few weeks,
and my pain subsided in a moment.
In the cold, she hardly had her wits to buzz,
No warning from either of us:
she sleeping in the richness of those petals,
then the hand, my hand, cupping the bloom
in devastating force, crushing the petals for the scent.
And she mortally threatened, wholly unaware
that I do this daily, alone with the gold last light
in what seems to me an act of love.

Juliet Patterson (b. 1963)

Index of First Lines

A slash of blue
Asphalt / colorless
Again the cry that
But she is / a stranger yet
By the time you read this
Coming late, as always
Darling,
Dear Alexa
Dear Alexa / I could / send you
Dear Alexa / I would / have liked
Dear friend / I regret to inform you
For love we all go
I'll send my / own two answers
Many times loneliness
No words / ripple like
Oh,
The things of which we want
The proof of those we knew before
There is another loneliness
We meet no stranger, but our self
We had not expected it
When I hoped / I feared / When I feared / I dared—
Where we / owe but / a little
You must let me / go first

ANCILLARY READINGS: *Open Me Carefully: Emily Dickinson's Intimate Letters to Susan Huntington Dickinson*; DEAN YOUNG'S POEM "IF THOU DISLIK'ST WHAT THOU FIRST LIGHT'ST ON."

Cullen Bailey Burns (b. 1964)

I Have Made a Paper Boat

and set words aflame upon water,
a message the lake
carries to the dead.

Fire (on water,
fire) on the last element
she knew,

bid her safe passage.

A wave, a kiss,
water lays down
the path.

KELLY EVERDING (B. 1964)

Omens

A cow lows three times.
Rats leave a house.
A cat spits at midnight,
and a white bird
smashes against a window.
An owl brings tidings.
Furniture creaks without cause.
A church bell strikes
while the parson intones his text.
Children born under a comet.

The lost wax from a candle
is a shroud.
A picture falls from its hook.
Meeting a goat unexpectedly.
A shrew runs across your foot.
January—bad for kings.
A shark following a ship
is a sure sign.

A dead man
knows what is going on
until the last spade-full of earth
touches his grave.
It is dangerous to walk away
and leave a book open.

Deidre Pope (b. 1965)

Anticipating Hoarfrost

It is after midnight, middle of November
and we decide to take a walk. This can't be
Minnesota, not with the air warm and fog
rising from the streets like tropical steam.

You tell me that as the temperature drops,
the fog will ice the trees, that everywhere
tomorrow will be hoarfrost, delicate
as petits fours or sparrow bones.

You say "hoar" and I hear "whore"—
wonder how I could have gone
so long without knowing of this:

how a name for *heat, open, red*
could come to describe
a breath of water, closed down
to rigidity: the desolate land's
ice white wrap.

Next day: we head south to walk
the river, and it is just as you said
it would be. The fog
is a bed-curtain pulled to reveal
the reeds: bright white feather boas
dropped from the shoulders,
an invitation into the sumac's
pulsing arms.

Pacyinz Lyfoung (b. 1969)

She No Zen

If the river yet to be born floats down in a snowflake
Spring yet to return whispers among browning leaves
Shuffling with the steps of an unconceived child
Unspeaking the secrets unshed
between what has already gone and what has yet to come

logged in the frozen desert of a woman half drowning
between jaded rocks cutting into her skin
in elusive waves polishing her dreams

stone skipping over her heartbeat
ricocheting on tortoise shells
sheathing the air she breathes in

defer to pulsating stars pooling
along the horizon dividing

darkness and dawn

Anna George Meek (b. 1969)

Democratic Vistas

> "...THE HUMAN FRAME, OR, ANY OBJECT IN THIS MANIFOLD
> UNIVERSE, IS BEST KEPT TOGETHER BY THE MIRACLE OF ITS OWN
> COHESION."
>
> —WALT WHITMAN, *DEMOCRATIC VISTAS*

We the materially sexed, shoulder-to-shoulder in mirrored offices,
have purpose to rage. Muscular, melancholy, we emigrate from our skins,
we whose debt is scraping the great ship's hull while we gather flimsy
    sympathies from on deck.
The chemical plant, the strip mine, the nuclear fission that would rend femur
    from cancerous femur, these multiply and divide,
and under our caress, the intimate government coos for its ghettos,
hangs its lovers in the public square. I am pregnant

with conflict, and colossal love, I am my own multitude.
Mexican, Laotian, Somali, Swedish, the crowds are outside, and within,
and they crave to hold the child, the real child emerging
from them. I would not know such wild, crushing happiness

but for the idea of country, divine aggregate, mutual attraction and aureole,
but for writers in a homeless shelter, letters from jail, an electrical charge
building in the human frame, but for the inflection of the crowds, our tongues,
our hands, warm in one another's, but for your interminable poems and your
    sweet, circular logic: Whitman, you fool.
How you make me love this body, after all.

April Lott (b. 1970)

Kitchen Sketch with Government Surplus

Sugar ghosts
across the bottom of its labeled bin.

Green pepper caps
slit to simulate
the empty gape of laughter.
Disillusionment
helps.

Water shouts:
one two free!
Add magic powder
to make sweet milk,
instant.

Rice hails
the walls of its little house.
Cornmeal dunes bury
evidence of the ant
skeletal with lack.

The depths of the icebox
harbor cheese,
long box of gold, everlast,
guarded

with engine growls
the dumb dog matches.

Katrina Vandenberg (b. 1971)

Record

Late night July, Minnesota,
John asleep on the glassed-in porch,
Bob Dylan quiet on a cassette

you made from an album
I got rid of soon after
you died. Years later,

I regret giving up
your two boxes of vinyl,
which I loved. Surely

they were too awkward,
too easily broken
for people who loved music

the way we did. But tonight
I'm in the mood for ghosts,
for sounds we hated: pop,

scratch, hiss, the occasional
skip. The curtains balloon;
I've got a beer; I'm struck

by guilt, watching you
from a place ten years away,
kneeling and cleaning each

with a velvet brush before
and after, tucking them in
their sleeves. Understand,

I was still moving then.
The boxes were heavy.
If I had known

I would stop here
with a husband to help me
carry, and room—too late,

the college kids pick over
your black bones on Mass. Ave.,
we'll meet again some day

on the avenue but still,
I want to hear it,
the needle hitting the end

of a side and playing silence
until the arm gives up,
pulls away.

Sun Yung Shin (b. 1974)

The Tourist's Prayer Bead Bracelet

> "And it's fine if you do light a lantern: that's like tossing
> a flower onto a piece of silk."
> —Venerable SongChol,
> Korean Chogye Zen Master and Patriarch

The thousands of carved buddhas forming the words *buddah* and *Ghandi* and other misplaced letters

The h goes missing...thanks becomes tanks...shit becomes sit...
shame becomes same...

It's simple to be a tourist
Tsirout, it's easy to slip into fake French in Korea

"Stacy's Mom" is playing in the taxi and we sing along
We sign, stringing the wristlet

Italicize the wrong language and you'll be eating dog for breakfast
Even the Korean flag has been assigned Pantone
Even flesh corresponds to Pantone
We can be programmed out of this silk knot

Repeté s'il vous plait:
These women are not my...
These women are not my...
These women are not my...

Stubbornly plural
All maintain a first-person point of view
None have agreed to be in my play or speak my dialogue

Broken-brick alleys marked with gray soapy water are not my tourist tears
Sentiments will not make me...
Repetitions will allow me to...

English words will never make me English
American words have done their work
I could not write the rules but I follow them like a tourist

A bar bracelet, permission to drink, permission to...
I will not haggle over the cost
You should take my money before I take it back

MAY M. LEE (B. 1979)

Keys

My mother doesn't think I should have keys,
but my brother Xin, who is three years younger than me, has keys.
He gets to come home whenever he wants to.
But I...I must knock.
Girls don't need keys, my mother said.
What for? Where are you going?
Nowhere, I think.
It is Xin who gives me his keys.
Just temporarily, he says. He can knock. Mom won't care.
But when she sees me opening the door into the house,
she tells me I must return them.
But I'm thinking that *I* need them too.
I need to be able to open and close doors when she's not around.
I need to be able to decide when I can come home.
I need to be trusted too.
And so I shake my head and I hold onto them,
these borrowed keys,
these keys that may take me somewhere, anywhere.

For Further Reading

Andrews, Jenné, et al, eds. *Women Poets of the Twin Cities: An Anthology*. Minneapolis: Vanilla Press, 1975.

Barron, Ron. *A Guide to Minnesota Writers*. Mankato, Minnesota: Minnesota Council of Teachers of English, 1987.

———. *A Guide to Minnesota Writers: Expanded and Revised*. Mankato, Minnesota: Minnesota Council of Teachers of English, 1993.

DeGrazia, Emilio and Monica DeGrazia. *33 Minnesota Poets*. Minneapolis: Nodin Press, 2000.

———. *26 Minnesota Writers*. Minneapolis: Nodin Press, 1995.

Densmore, Frances. *Chippewa Music*. Washington, D.C.: Government Printing Office. 1910.

———. *Chippewa Music—II*. Washington, D.C.: Government Printing Office. 1913.

Eastman, Elaine Goodale. *Sister to the Sioux: The Memoirs of Elaine Goodale Eastman, 1885-1891*. Edited by Kay Graber. Lincoln: University of Nebraska Press, 1978.

Erdrich, Heid E. and Laura Tohe. Editors. *Sister Nations: Native American Writers on Community*. Minneapolis: Minnesota Historical Society Press, 2002.

Fitz-Patrick, Nan, ed. *Minneapolis Skyline: Anthology of Minneapolis Poems*. Minneapolis: Minneapolis Poetry Circle, 1940.

Grounds for Peace: An Anthology of Writings by the Members of Women Against Military Madness and Women Poets of the Twin Cities. Minneapolis: Women Against Military Madness, 1994.

Hamerski, Susan Thurston, Beverly Voldseth and Karen Herseth Wee, eds. *Tremors, Vibrations, Enough to Rearrange the World: Northfield Women Poets*. Northfield, Minnesota: Blackhat Press, 1995.

Hedin, Robert, ed. *Where One Voice Ends Another Begins: 150 Years of Minnesota Poetry*. St. Paul: Minnesota Historical Society Press / Borealis Books, 2007.

Lauber, Peg Carlson, ed. *A Change in Weather: Midwest Women Poets*. Eau Claire, Wisconsin: Rhiannon Press, 1978.

Leighton, Louise, ed. *Poems of the Arrowhead*. Virginia, Minnesota: Virginia Writers' Club, 1936.

Miller, Susan Cummins. *A Sweet, Separate Intimacy: Women Writers of the American Frontier, 1800-1922*. Salt Lake City: University of Utah Press, 2000.

Minnesota Centennial Literature Group. Minnesota Statehood Centennial Commission. St. Paul, 1958.

Moore, James and Cary Waterman, eds. *Minnesota Writes: Poetry*. Minneapolis: Milkweed Editions/Nodin Press, 1987.

Moua, Mai Neng. *Bamboo Among the Oaks: Contemporary Writing by Hmong Americans*. St. Paul: Minnesota Historical Society Press, 2002.

Nute, Grace Lee. *A History of Minnesota Books and Authors*. Minneapolis: University of Minnesota Press, 1958.

Sargent, Theodore. *The Life of Elaine Goodale Eastman*. Lincoln: University of Nebraska Press, 2005.

Schilplin, Maude C., ed. *Minnesota Verse: An Anthology*. St. Cloud, Minnesota: The Times Publishing Co., 1934.

———, ed. *Minnesota Verse: An Anthology*. Rev. ed. St. Cloud, Minnesota: The Times Publishing Co., 1938.

Vinz, Mark and Thom Tammaro, eds. *Inheriting the Land: Contemporary Voices from the Midwest*. Minneapolis: University of Minnesota Press, 1993.

Vizenor, Gerald R. *Summer in the Spring: Ojibwe Lyric Poems and Tribal Stories*. Minneapolis: Nodin Press, 1981.

Wheeler, Sylvia Griffith, ed. *In the Middle: Ten Midwestern Women Poets: An Anthology of Poems, Statements, and Criticism*. Kansas City, Missouri: BkMk Press, 1985.

Yesner, Seymour, ed. *25 Minnesota Poets.* Minneapolis: Minneapolis Public Schools, 1974.

———, ed. *25 Minnesota Poets #2.* Minneapolis: Nodin Press, 1977.

Contributors

PATRICIA BARONE (B. 1943) is the author of *The Wind* and *Handmade Paper*. Her short stories have been published in *American Voices: Webs of Diversity*. She is a retired registered nurse and medical writer.

SANDY BEACH (B. 1955) has published poems in *Sojourn, Perigee, Poetry Motel, Sidewalks, ArtWord Quarterly*, and The National Museum of Women in the Arts Archives in Washington D.C. She is the recipient of a graduate residency to the Ezra Pound Center for Literature in Merano, Italy. She was a Loft-Mentorship participant in 2004-05, and has twice been awarded residencies at Norcroft. She received her M.F.A. at Hamline University.

HARRIET BISHOP (1817-1883) was born in Vermont and moved to St. Paul in 1847, two years before Minnesota became a territory, in response to a call from the missionary Thomas Williamson. A devout Baptist, Miss Bishop became Minnesota's first public school teacher, and her early classroom was a former blacksmith's shop, which was infested with vermin—snakes and rats—and the occasional chicken. She also started a Sunday school, which led to the first Baptist church in St. Paul. She was committed to women's suffrage and temperance, and felt that women had a moral obligation to provide a civilizing influence in the American frontier. She was instrumental in the formation of many civic groups, including the Ladies Christian Union. She married John McConkey in 1858, from whom she was later divorced. The excerpts used in this volume are part of *Minnesota, Then and Now*, a book-length poem published in 1869, describing the geographical features, towns and villages, and people of her beloved state. Bishop also wrote *Floral Home, or First Years in Minnesota*, which included early sketches of her life in St. Paul, published in 1857, and *Dakota War Whoop*, an account of conflicts between settlers, adventurers, and the Native people during the period of 1862-1863, which was published in 1864. The Minnesota History Center has collected considerable material on Harriet Bishop. She was an energetic reformer and an idealist.

CANDACE BLACK (B. 1955) is the author of *The Volunteer*. She is the recipient of a SASE/Jerome Foundation Fellowship and a Loft-McKnight Award. She teaches creative writing at Minnesota State University, Mankato.

LILY LAWRENCE BOW (1870-1943) was best known as a Dade County pioneer in Florida. There she moved in 1900 with her family after living in St. Paul, where her two children were born. She was a librarian and also an editor, publishing a quarterly magazine of verse called *Cycle* as well as poetry columns for local papers. She also sold citrus and raised chickens. It was largely through her efforts that a public library in Homestead, Florida, became a reality, and for years it occupied a corner in a women's club. In 1939 a permanent W.P.A. building was built and called the Lily Lawrence Bow Library. Most of her book and pamphlet publications came later in life, in the 1930s. They include *Wind in the Palm Trees Singing, Noel, Cycle Vignettes*, and *Wings and Things*, all in 1936 and 1937.

JILL BRECKENRIDGE (B. 1938) won The Bluestem Award, judged by William Stafford, for her book of poems, *How To Be Lucky* (1990). Her sequence of poetry and prose, *Civil Blood*, was nominated for the 1986 National Book Critics' Circle Award and was an American Library Association's Notable Book of the Year.

BETTY BRIDGMAN (1915-1999) "I do not consider that I ever wrote a worthwhile poem before taking a course in astronomy," wrote Betty Bridgman after she had won praise and second place in a poetry competition at her school, Hamline University, in 1936. Her name was then Elizabeth Klein, and the prize was called the Bridgman Poetry Prize, after the late President Emeritus of Hamline, George Henry Bridgman. Within a year, Elizabeth Klein had married his son, Donald Bridgman, and she went on to teach at Hamline and write poetry all her life. She published two books of poems in the 1950s: *This is Minnesota* and *Pioneers in Progress: Chorus for American Women*, and wrote essays for various magazines and newspapers, including the *Christian Science Monitor*—where the poems in this anthology first appeared—and *Ladies' Home Journal*. During World War II, she wrote three one-act plays, published by the Treasury Department, to promote the sale of war bonds. She had six children, and her son Art remembers that her favorite place in the natural world—which she loved—was "between the water and land because it was teeming with life." He also quoted his mother as saying, "The purpose of an artist is not to entertain or make people happy, but to crack the shell of the egg and make you think."

RUTH F. BRIN (B. 1921) is one of the foremost writers of interpretive Jewish liturgy and original Jewish-themed poetry in the United States. Rabbi Ira Eisenstein has called her "one of the few truly authentic Jewish poets, writing in English, in this country." Brin began writing innovative liturgy in the 1950s, well before the emergence of an organized Jewish feminist movement or the publication of gender-neutral prayer books. She is the author of three of volumes of poetry, including *Harvest: Collected Poems and Prayers*, eight children's books, and a memoir. Published in four poetry collections and five books of worship services, many of her poems have been incorporated into the prayer books of the Reform, Reconstructionist, and Conservative movements and included in many anthologies. She reviewed books for the *Minneapolis Star Tribune* for twenty-eight years and still writes reviews for *American Jewish World*.

CAROL RYRIE BRINK (1895-1981) was born in Moscow, Idaho, where her father Alexander Ryrie served as the town's first mayor. She said that she remembered her childhood as a happy one, though she lost her parents and grandfather at an early age. She was raised by her maternal grandmother, whom she adored, and her famous books, *Caddie Woodlawn* and *Magical Melons* were, she said, a retelling of her grandmother's childhood stories of her Wisconsin pioneer family. Carol Ryrie Brink graduated from the University of California in 1918, and married that same year, moving with her husband to St. Paul where he taught mathematics at the University of Minnesota. She had two children. When her husband had the opportunity to teach in Scotland, and later study and write in France with support from a Sheldon Traveling Fellowship from Harvard, the whole family embarked, and the years spent abroad were fruitful ones as she began to write and publish seriously, both poetry and stories for children. She was extremely successful, winning a Newbery Award for *Caddie Woodlawn* in 1936, and publishing poetry in the best periodicals, including *Poetry*, *The Gypsy*, and *The Commonweal*. In all she published over twenty-seven books and plays for both adults and children, and some of her later poems were collected in a 1978 hand-printed book called *Shreds and Patches*.

LUCILLE BRODERSON (B. 1916) is the author of two chapbooks of poetry, *Beware* and *A Thousand Years*. She has also been published in *33 Minnesota Poets*. A Minnesota native, born in Willmar, Broderson started taking creative writing classes at the University of Minnesota when she was in her 70s.

ALISON BROWN (1899-1949) was born and raised in Duluth and worked there as a St. Louis County welfare board case supervisor, having studied social work at the University of Chicago and the University of Minnesota. She wrote three books of poems: a book of verse for children called *The Candle Beams* (1919); *Songs of the Northland and Other Poems* (1923); and *Lake Superior Magic* (1927), from which the work in this volume was taken. One of her poems, "They Shall Not Pass," was set to music and became an Allied marching song during the First World War, and another composition, "The Lure of the Arrowhead," originally published in the local newspaper, was printed and distributed nationally in an edition of one million copies in conjunction with an industrial exposition in the Arrowhead region, a small irony as much of her poetry praises the beauty of the natural world.

She published frequently in the *Christian Science Monitor*, and was a member of First Church of Christ Scientist in Duluth.

BETSY BROWN (B. 1963) is the author of *Year of Morphines* (2002), a winner of the National Poetry Series. She received her M.F.A. from the University of Iowa Writer's Workshop. She currently lives in Minneapolis.

NELLIE MANLEY BUCK (1877-1968) abbreviated her mother's maiden name, Buckley, to form her nom de plume, which she used as a newspaper editor and poet. She was raised and lived on the Iron Range in Coleraine, where she edited the *Itasca Iron News* and was active in civic organizations, most notably the Coleraine Junior Women's Club. She only published one book of poems, *By Winding Trails* (1928), which was named after her newspaper poetry column. She was also responsible for a 1936 book of essays, excerpted from the newspaper, about hunting and fishing in the northland, called *Outdoors with "Dad" Lammon: Compiled and Published as a Distraction to Relieve the Tedium of the Great American Depression from the Office of the Itasca Iron News, Coleraine, Minn*. Nellie Manley Buck was one of the early active members of the League of Minnesota Poets.

CULLEN BAILEY BURNS (B. 1964) is the author of *Paper Boat* (2003), recipient of a 2004 Minnesota Book Awards commendation for best first book of poetry by a Minnesota writer. A 1999 recipient of a Minnesota State Arts Board Fellowship, she lives in Minneapolis and teaches at Century College.

MARISHA CHAMBERLAIN (B. 1952) is a poet, fiction writer, playwright and librettist. Her first collection of poems, *Powers*, was the winner of a New Rivers Press Minnesota Voices Project. Her plays have been staged throughout the United States, Canada, and Great Britain. She lives in Hastings, Minnesota.

SHARON CHMIELARZ (B. 1940) is the author of *The Rhubarb King* (2006), *The Other Mozart* (2001), *But I Won't Go Out in a Boat* (1991), and *Different Arrangements* (1983), all collections of poetry. Her books for children include *The Pied Piper of Hamlin* (1990) and *Down at Angel's* (1994).

MARIANNE CLARKE (1865-1948) was born and died in St. Cloud, Minnesota, though she traveled extensively. She was the daughter of pioneers in the area. She belonged to many civic organizations and was a charter member of the League of Minnesota Poets. Her books included *Miss America* (1928), and *Sunlit Trails* (1937), both published by New York presses. In 1917 she published a patriotic broadside called "A Letter to Sammie," part of a large body of writing which rose out of America's involvement in the First

World War, and she also wrote the lyrics for several state songs, including (in 1922) "Minnesota, the North Star State: Song for School and Home."

CLARA A. CLAUSEN (1880–1956) was born in Blooming Prairie, Minnesota, and educated at St. Mary's Hall in Faribault. She also attended school in Illinois and Ohio, and had a career as a teacher in Minnesota, North Dakota, South Dakota, and Ohio. She was one of the founders of the League of Minnesota Poets in 1934, was its first secretary/treasurer, and remained active in the organization for many years. She published widely in periodicals and newspapers, lectured on poetry, and taught poetry by correspondence. Poems in this volume are taken from her book *Silver Land*, published by *The Kenyon Leader* in Kenyon, Minnesota. She was also the author of several books on writing instruction, including *Steps in Creative Poetry* (1934) and *Words Divided and Hyphenated* (1931). In 1939 she published a poem in pamphlet form called *Raid on Northfield (September 7, 1876)*, an account of a bank robbery in that town by Frank and Jesse James.

GRACE NOLL CROWELL (1877–1969) wrote her first poem, called "The Marshland," in Farmington, Minnesota, in 1906. She was born in Iowa, and eventually settled with her husband in Texas, but much of her first book, *White Fire*, was written in Minnesota. She became a famous poet in the Texas of the twenties and thirties, eventually publishing over thirty-five books of poetry, prose devotions, and children's stories. It was said that at one point every home in Texas had a book of verse by Grace Noll Crowell. Her husband, who was in the oil business, eventually quit his job to manage her career. She was named Poet Laureate of Texas in 1935, and one of her books of patriotic verse was printed in an edition of hundreds of thousands of copies for distribution among soldiers in World War II. Praise for her verse came from the likes of Dale Carnegie, who called her "one of the most beloved poets in America." She herself said, "My sons are my three best poems." There have been modern reprints and collections of her verse, including a Harper and Row 1965 publication called *Poems of Inspiration and Courage: the Best Verse of Grace Noll Crowell*. A few of her many books include *Light of the Years* (1936), *Songs for Courage* (1938), *Songs of Hope* (1938), and *The Wind-Swept Harp* (1946), all from Harper and Brothers.

CAROL CONNOLLY (B. 1934) is the author of *Payments Due*, a collections of poems. She has worked as a columnist for the *Saint Paul Pioneer Press*, *Minneapolis-St. Paul* magazine, and *Minnesota's Journal of Law and Politics*. She has been a commentator for KARE Television, an NBC affiliate, and performed in *What's So Funny about Being Female?* at the Dudley Riggs Theatre in Minneapolis. She has served as co-chair of the Minnesota Women's Political Caucus, chair of the Saint Paul Human Rights Commission, and chair of the affirmative action committee of the Minnesota Racing Commission.

FLORENCE CHARD DACEY (B. 1941) is the author of two poetry collections, *The Swoon* and *The Necklace*, and the opera *Lightning*. She holds degrees in English and Education and has lived in Cottonwood, Minnesota, for thirty-five years.

FRANCES DENSMORE (1867-1957) was born in Red Wing, Minnesota, and as a child she heard the songs and drumming of Sioux settlements near her home along the Mississippi River, which fired her imagination. Her father was a surveyor and civil engineer in what was then the Northwest Frontier. She loved music and attended Oberlin Conservatory and later, Harvard, studying piano, organ, and music theory. This training served her well in what was to become her life's work and passion: the recording of Native American songs. After her education she returned to Red Wing and became a music teacher. However, she was increasingly drawn to and intrigued by Native American songs, and saw them as a rapidly vanishing treasure. She took her first notes on the songs of Good Bear Woman at the Prairie Island Dakota Reservation in 1903. During the next few years her efforts became more organized, and she acquired funding and wax cylinder recording equipment. With support from the Smithsonian Institution's Bureau of American Ethnology, she spent the next thirty years and more, first in Minnesota, and later all across the country, recording songs and pictographs, collecting artifacts, and taking notation from singers of many tribes. She did her best work among the Sioux and Ojibwe in Minnesota and the Dakotas. This volume contains "Ojibwe Love-charm Songs," a sample of her collected Native American work from *Chippewa Music*, originally published in 1910 and 1913 by the Smithsonian Institution, and also one of her own poems. She is best known for her ethnological recordings. She lived with her sister in the family home in Red Wing for more than a half-century, eventually selling the house after her sister's death and taking a room in a boarding house. She died in 1957 at the age of 90. Today she is a controversial figure as she reflected many of the attitudes of her era; however, her recordings still generate intense interest.

MARGARETTE BALL DICKSON (1884-1963). Few writers of the early Twentieth Century in Minnesota, male or female, can match Margarette Ball Dickson Haining Jensen for industry and vigor. She served as Minnesota Poet Laureate in 1934, was president of the League of Minnesota Poets, editor of *The Country Bard*, and officer or active member of dozens of civic and literary organizations at a local and national level. Born in Iowa, she traveled, taught, and lectured in many places, even serving as a rural school teacher among the Sioux in Sisseton, South Dakota. She settled in Staples, Minnesota, in 1931, and established the Dickson-Haining School of Creative Writing with her husband, John Haining, who wrote short stories and was known as the "Northern Pacific Bard." Among her many books are:

Tumbleweeds (1926), *Gumbo Lilies* (1924), *One Man and a Dream* (1937), and *Fuel of One Flame* (1955). She also edited several anthologies, including *The Owl* (1928), *Book of Father Verse* (1941), *Patterns for Poems* (1937), *More Patterns for Poems* (1941), and *Added Patterns for Poems* (1954). These last three were comprehensive illustrations of various poetic forms. According to anthologist Maude Schilplin, one of Dickson's poems, "Night on the Dunes," was written in a form that became known as the "Dickson Nocturne."

KIRSTEN DIERKING (B. 1962) is the author of *One Red Eye* and *Northern Oracle*. She is the recipient of a Minnesota State Arts Board Fellowship in Poetry, and a Career Initiative Grant from The Loft Literary Center. She received an M.A. in Liberal Studies with a concentration in creative writing from Hamline University, and teaches at Anoka-Ramsey Community College.

NORITA DITTBERNER-JAX (B. 1944) is the author of *What They Always Were*, winner of a New Rivers Press Minnesota Voices Project in 1995. Her work is included in *33 Minnesota Poets*. She is the Secondary Language Arts Coordinator for Saint Paul Public Schools.

ELAINE GOODALE EASTMAN (1863-1953) and her younger sister Dora published several books of poems together while they were still children. Elaine's poem, "Ashes of Roses," written when she was eleven, was widely anthologized and set to music, and the sisters' poetry about the Berkshire flora and their young lives at Sky Farm captured the interest of the reading public nationally, and their books went through many editions. At the age of twenty, Elaine traveled to the Hampton Institute in Virginia to train to be a teacher of Native Americans, some of whom boarded there. She traveled the next year to the Dakota Territory and began a day school near a Sioux village. She became fluent in the Sioux language, traveled with the Sioux, and was appointed the first superintendent of schools in Dakota by then President Harrison. Elaine Goodale met Charles Eastman, a Sioux physician trained at Dartmouth, while tending survivors of the Wounded Knee massacre. With him she wrote several books of Sioux legends and also served as his amanuensis as his fame grew as a speaker. She also raised six children. They lived in St. Paul for a number of years, and two of her children were born there. After thirty years of marriage they separated, and Elaine carried on her career as a writer near Amherst, Massachusetts. A new biography of her life has recently appeared, and she herself wrote of her life as a school teacher in Dakota in her memoir, *Sister to the Sioux*. Her last book of poems, *The Voice at Eve*, was published in 1930. She is chiefly known for her early verse: *All Around the Year: Verses from Sky Farm; Apple-blossoms: Verses of Two Children*; her work with her husband, particularly *Wigwam Evenings: Sioux Folk Tales Retold*, and her biography, *Pratt, the Red Man's Moses*, although she also wrote essays, poems, articles, and an autobiographical novel, *One Hundred Maples*, published in 1935.

MARY HENDERSON EASTMAN (1818-1887) is known for her two major works, *Dacotah; or Life and Legends of the Sioux Around Fort Snelling*, published in 1849, and *Aunt Phillis' Cabin; or, Southern Life As It Is*, published in 1852. She is also known as the wife of the painter Seth Eastman, whose portraits of native villages and customs were considered almost photographic in their accuracy. The poems in this volume are taken from *Dacotah*, which contains essays and poetry based on firsthand observations of Sioux culture from her years living in Fort Snelling and traveling the frontier, and a small book she wrote called *Jenny Wade of Gettysburg*, a sentimental ballad describing a Civil War bystander, Jenny Wade, a baker of bread for the foot soldiers, caught up in battle because she refused to leave her ovens and her duty, a decision that proved fatal. Mary Eastman was Seth's second wife; his first was a Sioux who bore him a daughter. This daughter was raised by her Sioux grandmother and, when grown, married a Sioux brave and bore a son who eventually took the name Charles Eastman, after his grandfather Seth. We mention this because another poet in this volume, Elaine Goodale, married this Charles Eastman more than a generation later. Mary Henderson Eastman was born in 1818 in Warrenton, Virginia, and her book *Aunt Phillis's Cabin* was an answer to Harriet Beecher Stowe's *Uncle Tom's Cabin*. It sold eighteen thousand copies in a matter of weeks after it appeared, and it argues that slavery is a "necessary evil" and uses, as was common during her time, biblical justifications for its continuance. Both of her major books have been recently reprinted, arguing for the historical significance of her observations, if not their moral currency.

HEID ERDRICH (B. 1963) is the author of two collections of poems, *The Mother's Tongue* (2005) and *Fishing for Myth* (1997) and a young adult novel, *Maria Tallchief* (1992). She is also the editor of the anthology *Sister Nations: Native American Women Writers on Community* (2002). She lives in St. Paul, where she is professor of Writing and Native American Literature at the University of St. Thomas.

LOUISE ERDRICH (B. 1954) is the author of more than fifteen novels, collections of short stories, children's books, and nonfiction. Her novel *Love Medicine*, was the recipient of the National Book Critics Circle Award, and *The Last Report on the Miracles at Little No Horse* was a finalist for the National Book Award. Her collections of poetry include *Jacklight*, *Baptism of Desire*, and *Original Fire: Selected and New Poems*. She lives in Minneapolis and is the founder and owner of the bookstore BirchBark Books.

MARY CUMMINGS EUDY (1874-1952) lived in Minneapolis, and later New York City, where she was a fashion designer as well as a poet. She designed clothing for, among others, Franklin D. Roosevelt's mother. She is the author of several broadsides and two major books of poems, *Quarried Crystals and Other Poems*, published by G.P. Putnam's Sons, and *Quicken the Current*, published by Harper & Brothers in New York. She also wrote a poem called "Oxen" that was set to music and taken up as a standard choral piece of the Great Depression. Her poems appeared in the best periodicals of the day, including *Harper's*, *Scribner's*, and *The Lyric*. Critics compared her to Emily Dickinson because her poems are most often concise, spare, interior. Mary Cummings Eudy died in New York City but was buried in Kentucky where she was born. In the introduction to *Quicken the Current*, Hugh Walpole has this to say about the poems: "They are marvels of compactness, like full teeming seeds.... The reader forgets that these poems are verbal—they might be in Persian; they might be precious stones, or geometry.... We have no sense of time, person, place, or gender; they could be contemporary with Manley Hopkins or Li Po or Herrick or they could—as they do—belong to the future."

KELLY EVERDING (B. 1964) is the author of the chapbook *Strappado for the Devil*. She lives in Minneapolis and works for *Rain Taxi*, a nonprofit literary organization.

NANCY FITZGERALD (B. 1943) is the author of three chapbooks of poetry. She contributed editorial assistance to *The Cancer Poetry Project*, which won a Minnesota Book Award in 2002. She taught creative writing for many years at the College of St. Scholastica in Duluth, and is now retired.

NAN FITZ-PATRICK (1883-1975) was one of the founding members of the League of Minnesota Poets in 1934, and she served the organization in many capacities over the next decades. In 1938 she succeeded Margarette Ball Dickson as president of the League, and she edited several of its publications, including an anthology, *Minneapolis Skyline* (1940), the League periodical called *The Moccasin*, and, with co-editor Robert Cary, a historical sketch of the group and its members in 1946. Her own poems were published in hundreds of newspaper poetry columns and general interest magazines, and she wrote two books, *Winding Road* (1945), from which the poems in this volume are taken, and *Far Horizons* (1957). In the 1957 issue of *The Moccasin*, she gives aspiring poets "Suggestions for Checking Poetry Technique," some of which include, "Do not use awkward inversions: angels absent are; roses red; tulips tall"...and "Adhere strictly to meter chosen." She was a child actress and remained interested in the theater. She said, "I have written poetry and short stories since childhood making booklets of wrapping paper sewed with string. My first efforts were limited in length only by the amount of paper on hand."

MARGOT FORTUNATO GALT (B. 1942) is the author of *Between the Houses, The Country's Way with Rain, The Story in History*, and *Turning the Feather Around*. She teaches at Hamline University and the University of Minnesota. She lives in St. Paul.

NANCY FREDERIKSEN (B. 1948) is the author of two poetry books: *Coming Up for Air*, and *Making Her Way: The Search for Helga*. She co-edited *Sidewalks*, a magazine of poetry, short stories, and artwork from 1991-2000. She is former Writer-in-Residence at Banfill Locke Center for the Arts in Fridley, Minnesota. She works as a paralegal for Zappia & LeVahn, Ltd., Fridley, and managing director of Minnesota Guitar Society in Minneapolis, Minnesota.

DIANE GLANCY (B. 1941) is a professor at Macalester College in St. Paul, where she has taught Native American literature and creative writing. She is the author of more than twenty collections of poetry, plays, short fiction, nonfiction, and novels. Her most recent collection of poetry is *Asylum in the Grasslands*.

VICKI GRAHAM (B. 1950) is currently an associate professor of English and creative writing at the University of Minnesota, Morris, where she has been teaching since 1989. Her chapbook, *Alembic*, was a finalist for the Minnesota Book Award in 2001. She has also published critical articles on poetry, literature and the environment.

HAZEL HALL (1886-1924) was born in St. Paul, moving as a child to Portland, Oregon. She is included in this volume, though she spent the rest of her days in Portland, because of our small Minnesota claim and because her poems are of such remarkable quality. At the age of twelve, after suffering from scarlet fever and possibly a fall, Hazel Hall was confined to a wheelchair for the rest of her life. She took up sewing to supplement the family income, and later, in her twenties, she turned to poetry as her eyesight began to fail. She wrote about sewing, about the people she saw passing in the street below her window, about disappointment and death—in short, about her own life. Her poems were embraced by readers and critics alike. William Braithwaite, writing for *The Boston Evening Transcript*, praised her highly: "Hazel Hall reminds me more of Emily Dickinson than any woman who has written poetry in America." Harriet Monroe published her in *Poetry* and gave a group of her needlework poems the "Young Poet's Prize." She died at the age of 38, but in the space of about a decade she produced three remarkable books: *Curtains* in 1921 and reprinted in 1922,

Walkers in 1923, and *Cry of Time* in 1928. Her last poem, "Slow Death," was published two weeks after her death in *The New Republic*. *The Collected Poems of Hazel Hall*, a collection of all the poems in her three books, appeared in 2000 from Oregon State University Press, edited and with an introduction by John Witte.

PATRICIA HAMPL (B. 1946) is the author of two collections of poetry, *Woman Before an Aquarium* and *Resort and Other Poems*. Her other books include two memoirs, *A Romantic Education* and *Virgin Time*, and a collection of nonfiction, *I Could Tell You Stories*. Two forthcoming books are *Blue Arabesque: In Search of the Sublime*, and *The Florist's Daughter*. She is Regents Professor at the University of Minnesota and a faculty member for the Prague Summer Program.

PHEBE HANSON (B. 1928) is the author of two books of poetry: *Sacred Hearts* and *Why Still Dance*. Her many awards include a Jerome Fellowship and a Bush Foundation Literary Fellowship.

JOANNE HART (B. 1927) is the author of *Witch Tree*, a collaboration with visual artist Hazel Belvo. She lives in the woods near the Pigeon River on the Grand Portage Chippewa Indian Reservation in Grand Portage, Minnesota.

MARGARET HASSE (B. 1950) is the author of two collections of poetry, *Stars Above, Stars Below* and *In a Sheep's Eye, Darling*. Originally from South Dakota, she moved to Minnesota in 1973 after graduating from Stanford University. For more than fifteen years, she was involved as a teaching poet with programs such as Arts & Corrections, COMPAS Writers in the Schools, and The Loft.

MAURINE HATHAWAY (1883/4-?) was born in Nebraska into an old settler family on her mother's side and, on her father's side, into the family of explorer Jacques Cartier, who discovered the St. Lawrence River. She attended Normal College in Cedar Falls, Iowa, business college in Minneapolis, and at the University of Colorado, where she studied journalism and creative writing. She was widowed shortly after marriage, and taught for several years and was a court reporter in Minnesota, living for many years in Minneapolis. She wrote three books of poems: *Embers* (1911), *Lyrics* (1912), and *Passion Lyrics* (1922); the poems in this volume are taken from the last of these. Stylistically, she was influenced by her contemporary, Edna St. Vincent Millay. She also wrote stories for children, and sold many verses to the Gibson Art Company of Cincinnati, which published broadsides, postcards, and lithographs. She returned to Nebraska to care for her mother, but continued to publish and was active there in women's and civic organizations.

SUSAN CAROL HAUSER (B. 1942) is the author of *Outside after Dark: New and Selected Poems; You Can Write a Memoir*; four natural history books; and several essay collections. She has twice received a Minnesota Book Award, is a Charter Resident at the Anderson Center for Interdisciplinary Studies, and is a recipient of a Jerome Foundation Travel and Study Grant, among other awards. She is a professor of English at Bemidji State University.

ANNA AUGUSTA VON HELMHOLTZ-PHELAN (1880-1964). Modern students of English at the University of Minnesota can apply for the Anna Augusta Von Helmholtz-Phelan scholarship, named in honor of this remarkable scholar and social activist. She was the author of *The Social Philosophy of William Morris* (Duke University Press, 1927) and *The Indebtedness of Samuel Taylor Coleridge to August Wilhelm von Schlegel* (University of Wisconsin, 1907, and reprinted in 1969 by Folcroft Press and in 1971 by Haskell House, New York), as well as a book of poems, *The Crystal Cup* (1949, Delta Phi Lambda, University of Minnesota). In the *Who's Who Among Minnesota Women*, compiled by Mary Dillon Foster in 1924, the entry for Anna Augusta Von Helmholtz-Phelan lists the many civic organizations to which she belonged and in which she was very active. Special interests were the women's suffrage movement, child welfare, and the working conditions of the poor, especially working women, conservation, and "promotion of dramatics." She was a member of the Equal Suffrage Club and a member of the state committee to determine minimum wages. Foster notes: "She is a Republican."

KATE LYNN HIBBARD (B. 1956) is the author of *Sleeping Upside Down*. She teaches at Minneapolis Community Technical College. Her awards include a McKnight Artist Fellowship, a Minnesota State Arts Board Grant, a Jerome Foundation Grant, and a residency at Hedgebrook.

EVA HOOKER (B. 1941) is Regents Professor of Poetry at Saint John's University, Collegeville, Minnesota, where she teaches Shakespeare, poetry writing, and Symposium, a seminar for first year students. She is the author of *The Winter Keeper*, a finalist for the Minnesota Book Award in poetry in 2001. She is a Sister of the Holy Cross.

JEAN JACOBSON (B. 1948) has contributed poems to the *New Yorker*, *The New Republic*, *Shenandoah*, and other magazines. She is the recipient of two Mirrelees/Stenger Fellowships at Stanford University, as well as the Bush Artist's Fellowship, and a Minnesota State Arts Board grant. She lives and works in Duluth, where she makes her living as an editor at the University of Minnesota.

DIANE JARVENPA (B. 1959) is the author of *Ancient Wonders: The Modern World*
and *Diving the Landscape*. She is also a singer, songwriter, guitarist, and a ver-
satile performer of folk and world music. As Diane Jarvi, she has recorded
five CDs of her music. Jarvi plays the 5-, 8-, 10-, 15-, and 36- string
kantele (Finnish folk harp). Her recordings have led to radio play and
performances at festivals in the U.S. and in Finland, where she is known as
Minnesotan Satakieli—"The Minnesota Nightingale."

DEBORAH KEENAN (B. 1950) is the author of *Household Wounds, One Angel
Then, The Only Window That Counts, Happiness*, and *Good Heart*. She has received
two Bush Fellowships for Poetry, an NEA fellowship for poetry, and a
Loft-McKnight Poet of Distinction Grant. She is a three-time Professor
of the Year award winner and teaches in the M.F.A. program at Hamline
University.

ATHENA KILDEGAARD (B. 1959) is the author of *Rare Momentum*, a collec-
tion of poems. She lives in Morris, Minnesota.

PATRICIA KIRKPATRICK (B. 1949) is the author of *Century's Road* and a
chapbook, *Orioles*, as well as three books for young readers: *Plowie: A Story
from the Prairie; Voices in Poetry: Maya Angelou;* and *Voices in Poetry: John Keats*. Among
her numerous awards are Fellowships from the National Endowment for
the Arts, the Bush Foundation, the Loft, The Minnesota Arts Board, and
the Jerome Foundation. She teaches in the M.F.A. program at Hamline
University where she is the poetry editor for *Water~Stone Review*.

KATHRYN KYSAR (B. 1960) is the author of *Dark Lake*. Her poems have ap-
peared in several literary magazines and have been featured on "A Writer's
Almanac." She teaches composition, creative writing and literature at
Anoka-Ramsey Community College in Coon Rapids, Minnesota.

JULIE LANDSMAN (B. 1944) has taught writing, literature, and educa-
tion at Carleton College and Hamline University, in addition to teaching
in public schools for twenty-eight years. She has published two critically
acclaimed books about her teaching experiences: *Basic Needs: A Year With Street
Kids in a City School*, recipient of a Minnesota Book Award, and *A White Teacher
Talks About Race*. She has co-edited two books for young people, one with
the novelist David Haynes. Her essays on education appear frequently in
national publications. She recently won a Loft Career Initiative Grant. Her
short story "Suspension" won the 2005 *New Letters* Award in Fiction.

MAY M. LEE (B. 1979). Hmong writer and community activist, May
Lee has published in the *Paj Ntaub Voice, Bamboo Among the Oaks*, and *Unarmed
Journal*. She is the recipient of a 2005 Loft Mentor in Non-Fiction award,

a Minnesota State Arts Board Artist Initiative Grant, and a Playwright Center Many Voices Fellowship. In 2001, she received the University of Minnesota's Anna Augusta von Helmholtz Phelan Scholarship for Creative Writing. She lives in St. Paul.

LOUISE LEIGHTON (1891-1974). Poet, editor, mother, newspaper woman, teacher, Louise Leighton was born in Milwaukee, Wisconsin. She came from a family (Purdy) that traced its lineage to three soldiers who fought in the American Revolution. She herself had three sons who fought in World War II. She wrote a group of extraordinary poems about war and peace, two of which we include in this volume, that were published in her 1953 book, *Journey to Light*, and that are strikingly contemporary and full of passion. She lived in Minnesota for many years, first in Minneapolis and later in Virginia and Hibbing, where she wrote for the newspaper, raised five children, and helped found the League of Minnesota Poets, The Range Writer's Club, and the Virginia Creative Writing group. In the 1950s, after moving to Baraboo, she founded the Wisconsin Fellowship of Poets. She edited several anthologies of verse for these organizations, and served them in leadership roles. Her books are *Journey to Light*, 1953, and *The Great Carrying Place* (Harbinger House, New York, 1944), a volume of historical verse about the explorer Pierre Radisson, a portion of which we have included in these pages.

MERIDEL LESUEUR (1900-1996) was born in Murray, Iowa, and grew up with the people and places of the political left. Her mother was a college instructor and her stepfather, Arthur LeSueur, was a lawyer and founder of the Industrial Workers of the World. The LeSueur family associated with figures such as Eugene Debs, Lincoln Steffens, and Emma Goldman, and they belonged to groups such as the Wobblies, the Populists, and the Farmers Alliance. As early as 1914, she participated in protests, marching with the survivors of the Ludlow mineworker massacre, and by 1924 she had joined the Communist Party. LeSueur's education was eclectic: when she went to New York to study at the American Academy of Dramatic Arts, she lived with the feminist Emma Goldman. At Mabel Dodge's literary salon she met Theodore Dreiser and Edna St. Vincent Millay. LeSueur was an original and mostly self-taught writer, and her short stories, experimental prose, novels and poems are filled with a wonderful combination of detailed observation, and idealism. She wrote about the down-and-out places of the Midwest, about unemployment and breadlines. She published her first story in 1927, and her prose and poetry were often seen in publications from *Vogue* and *True Confessions* to the literary journal *Dial*, until the McCarthy era when she was blacklisted and the only places that would publish her work were the small journals of the extreme left. Her best-known title, *The Girl*, which at first appeared only in the form of excerpts in a few of the radical journals, is an example of her originality. The entire book is a transcription of things LeSueur heard women say in the Workers Alliance. The dialogue is without quotation marks and captures the feel of hardscrabble street life. Despite harassment and discrimination, LeSueur continued to write and began writing for children, producing a series of highly praised lyrical biographies, with titles such as *Nancy Hanks of Wilderness Road: A Story of Abraham Lincoln's Mother*. She also began exploring the legends and symbols of Native American cultures, which came to play a large part in the volume of her poems, *Rites of Ancient Ripening*, from which we take our selection. She kept on writing into her 90s.

ROSEANN LLOYD (B. 1944) is the author of *Because of the Light* and *War Baby Express*. Her first collection of poetry, *Tap Dancing for Big Mom*, won the Minnesota Voices Competition in 1985. She co-edited *Looking for Home: Women Writing about Exile*, recipient of an American Book Award in 1991. She also translated the contemporary Norwegian novel, *The House with the Blind Glass Windows*, by author Herbjørg Wassmo.

MARY LOGUE (B. 1952) has published three collections of poetry: *Discriminating Evidence, Settling*, and *Meticulous Attachment*. Her other publishing credits include a book about her grandmother, *Halfway Home*, and nine children's books, including the young adult novel *Dancing with an Alien*. She also has published six mysteries—*Red Lake of the Heart, Still Explosion*, and four in the Claire Watkins series: *Blood Country, Dark Coulee, Glare Ice*, and *Bone Harvest*. *Snatched*, first in a series of young adult mysteries, is co-authored with Pete Hautman. She has taught writing at The Loft in Minneapolis and Hamline University in St. Paul for many years, and has served as an editor for book publishers, journals, and magazines.

LILY LONG (1862-1927) was born in St. Paul, the daughter of Reverend Peter Long. She was educated in private schools and the University of Wisconsin, then returned to St. Paul and lived with her sister on Summit Avenue. She wrote two novels, *A Squire of Low Degree* and *Apprentices to Destiny*, and many short stories, as well as a mystery series under the nom de plume Roman Doubleday. Her poetry was highly regarded, and she published in the finest journals of the day, including *The Atlantic Monthly, The Bellman, Poetry, Harper's, McCall's*, and *McClure's*. For two years she was literary editor of the *St. Paul Pioneer Press*. When the society women of the St. Paul of 1911 decided to stage a pageant illustrating the history of the great state of Minnesota through poetry and tableau, it was Lily Long who wrote the historical verse that was recited during the program in the auditorium of the St. Paul Institute. Her books of poetry are *Radisson, The Voyageur*, a four-act drama in verse (Henry Holt Publishers, 1914), and *The Singing Place and Other Poems* (1922).

APRIL LOTT (B. 1970) received her MFA from the University of Virginia. She is a graduate of the Cave Canem Summer Workshop Retreat for Black Poets. She was a recipient of a Minnesota State Arts Board Fellowship in 2003.

PACYINZ LYFOUNG (B. 1969) is an activist, artist, a legal attorney, and a co-founding executive director of a Pan Asian battered women's program and shelter. She is a state agency fair housing policy specialist. She has received an Asian Pacific American Women's Leadership Institute Fellowship, a St. Paul Companies' Leadership in Neighborhood Grant, Hmong Women's Action Team Courage Award, a Loft Inroads for Emerging Asian Pacific Islanders Writers Fellowship, and a Jerome Fellowship. She volunteers her time to address women's issues and believes in art as another tool for social change.

FREYA MANFRED (B. 1944) is the author of five collections of poetry; *My Only Home, A Goldenrod Will Grow, Yellow Squash Woman, American Roads,* and *Flesh and Blood,* and a memoir, *Fredrick Manfred: A Daughter Remembers.*

LINDA BACK MCKAY (B. 1947) is the author of *Ride That Full Tilt Boogie* and *Shadow Mothers: Stories of Adoption and Reunion.* She is an instructor at the Loft and works as a teaching artist throughout Minnesota and South Dakota.

ETHNA MCKIERNAN (B. 1951) is the author of *The One Who Swears You Can't Start Over.* She is the owner of Irish Books and Media in Minneapolis.

ANNA GEORGE MEEK (B. 1969) is the author of *Acts of Contortion,* the 2002 recipient of the Brittingham Prize for Poetry. She holds graduate degrees from the writing seminars at the Johns Hopkins University and Indiana University. She is also a freelance violinist, violin teacher, and instructor at the Loft Literary Center in Minneapolis.

MARTHA GEORGE MEEK (B. 1942) is the author *Rude Noises,* a chapbook of poems. With Jay Meek, she is the editor of *Prairie Volcano,* the first anthology of poetry and fiction by North Dakota writers. Having founded the non-profit St. Ives Press, she became editor and publisher of *In Kind,* poems in celebration of poet Phillip Booth's 70th birthday. She has been a resident scholar at the Ecumenical Institute at St. John's University in Collegeville, Minnesota. She also served as book review editor for the *North Dakota Quarterly.* She is retired as a professor of English from the University of North Dakota and lives in Minneapolis.

LESLIE ADRIENNE MILLER (B. 1956) is the author of *Eat Quite Everything You See, Yesterday Had a Man In It, Ungodliness, Staying Up For Love*, and *The Resurrection Trade*, a forthcoming collection of poems in 2007. She is a Professor of English at the University of St. Thomas in St. Paul.

GRACE FALLOW NORTON (1876-1956) was born in Northfield. Her mother died when she was eleven, and she subsequently lived with a sister before marrying George Macrum, who was a well-known artist and whose works are collected by museums. They traveled a good deal, living in Europe for a time before moving to Sloatsburg, New York. Grace Fallow Norton was widely and seriously published, with five books of poetry from Houghton Mifflin, poems set to music, broadsides widely distributed, poems anthologized, work placed in the most respected periodicals in the country, such as *Poetry, The Atlantic Monthly*, and *Harper's*. Harriet Monroe admired her work and included it in collections she put together from the pages of *Poetry* magazine. Her books of poetry include *Little Gray Songs from St. Joseph's* (1912), *The Sister of the Wind* (1914), *Roads* (1916), *What is Your Legion* (1916), and *The Miller's Youngest Daughter* (1924).

MONICA OCHTRUP (B. 1942) is the author two collections of poems, *What I Cannot Say/ I Will Say* and *Pieces from the Long Afternoon*. She is the recipient of a Loft-McKnight Award of Distinction in poetry. She lives in St. Paul, where she works as a writer's consultant.

MARY ROSE O'REILLEY (B. 1944) teaches English at the University of St. Thomas in St. Paul. Her books include *The Peaceable Classroom, Radical Presence, The Garden at Night*, and *The Barn at the End of the World: The Apprenticeship of a Quaker, Buddhist Shepherd*. Her collection of poetry, *Half Wild*, received the 2005 Walt Whitman Award from the National Academy of American Poets.

ELIZABETH ONESS (B. 1960) is the author of the novel *Departures* (2004) and *Articles of Faith*, winner of the 2000 Iowa Short Fiction Prize. She teaches at Winona State University.

MARTHA OSTENSO (1900-1963), the famous novelist, began her writing career as a poet. Her first published book, *A Far Land* (1924, Thomas Seltzer, New York), was a book of poetry and contains the work we have included in this volume. In 1925, her novel *Wild Geese* was published, and in 1926 it won a $13,500 prize from Dodd, Mead, and Co. and was eventually made into a movie. In all, Martha Ostenso wrote twenty-five novels, many about farm life in Minnesota. She was born in Bergen, Norway, and came to America with her family at the age of two. She lived as a child, she says, "in seven little towns in Minnesota and South Dakota. Towns of the field and prairie, all, redolent of the soil from which they had sprung and eloquent of that struggle common to the farmer the world over...seven mean, yet glorious little towns...." She attended the University of Manitoba, taught school in rural Manitoba, studied novel writing at Columbia University in 1921-22, and returned to Minnesota in 1923, living in Minneapolis and then Gull Lake in Cass County from 1923 to 1963. Her 1943 novel, *O River, Remember!*, was set in the Minnesota Red River Valley, and was a Literary Guild choice that year. For many years she lived with novelist Douglas Durkin, and they married in 1945.

SHEILA PACKA (B. 1956) is the author of the chapbook *Always Saying Good-Bye*. She holds an M.F.A. in creative writing and is an adjunct writing teacher at Lake Superior College. In 1975, she worked at U.S. Steel's Minntac mine. She has been the recipient of Loft-McKnight Awards in both poetry and prose.

NANCY PADDOCK (B. 1942) is the author of *A Dark Light*. Her poems have appeared in many literary magazines and anthologies. She has worked for the COMPAS Writers and Artists in the Schools program.

JULIET PATTERSON (B. 1963) is the author of *The Truant Lover*. She was a volunteer educator with the Minnesota Advocates for Human Rights and with the United Cambodian Association of Minnesota Youth Programs. She teaches poetry and creative writing at the College of St. Catherine, Hamline University, The Loft Literary Center, the Perpich Center for Arts Education, and Banfill-Locke Arts Center.

IRENE PAULL (1908-1981) was born and raised in Duluth, the daughter of Russian Jews with roots in the village of Peryaslov. She traveled to Chicago as a young woman, but returned to Duluth to marry Hank Paull, who became a labor lawyer there. They were both extremely active politically, and Irene, with activist Sam Davis, founded the *Timber Worker* newspaper, which would become *Midwest Labor*. During the 1930s Woody Guthrie and Pete Seeger stayed with the Paull family when they passed through Duluth. In 1947, when Irene's two children were nine and fourteen, Hank Paull died of a sudden heart attack. She never remarried. She joined the Communist Party and continued to work for a variety of social causes, including civil rights, women's rights, and labor issues. She published many essays and poems, especially in *Midwest Labor* (Duluth), *Minnesota Labor* (Minneapolis), and *Jewish Currents* (New York), and was widely anthologized. Irene Paull was a close friend of fellow poet Meridel LeSueur, who wrote the preface to the 1996 book *Irene: Selected Writings of Irene Paull*, published by Midwest Villages and Voices of Minneapolis.

WANG PING (B. 1957) was born in Shanghai and grew up on a small island in the East China Sea. After three years of farming in a mountain village, she attended Beijing University. In 1985 she left China to study in the U.S., earning her Ph.D. from New York University. Her collections of poetry include *Of Flesh and Spirit* (1998) and *The Magic Whip* (2003). She edited and co-translated *New Generation: Poetry from China Today* (1999), an anthology of Chinese poetry. Other publications include *American Visa*, a collection of short stories; *Foreign Devil*, a novel; and a cultural study, *Aching for Beauty: Footbinding in China*. She has received awards from the National Endowment for the Arts, the Bush Foundation, and the Minnesota State Arts Board. She lives in St. Paul and teaches at Macalester College.

DEIDRE POPE (B. 1965) is the author of *Let's Investigate: Sharks*. She earned an M.F.A. in Poetry from Cornell University and her B.A. from Wells College. Her poems have appeared in numerous literary journals and anthologies.

EDRIS MARY PROBSTFIELD (1907-1980) was born in Moorhead, Minnesota, and grew up on a farm north of the town. Her grammar school education took place in Moorhead, and she graduated from Moorhead High School in 1923. After that, she alternated between taking classes at North Dakota State College in Fargo and teaching in rural Montana, finishing her B.S. in Education in 1929 and teaching English in Havana, North Dakota, and in Fargo. In 1936, she married Raymond H. Hack. During the thirties, her poems appeared in *Poetry, The Rectangle, The Lantern, Southern Literary Review, The Poet*, and in several anthologies, including *American Women Poets* in 1937. The poems included in this anthology are taken from a collection of her poems which appeared under the title *Open Windows*, published in 1933. An earlier collection, *Between Sleeps*, was published in 1926. Her grandfather, Randolph Probstfield, was one of the earliest settlers in the Red River Valley, and is buried in the Prairie Home Cemetery (the inspiration for the name of Garrison Keillor's radio show *Prairie Home Companion*) in Moorhead, Minnesota. Edris Mary wrote a fictionalized account of her grandfather's history, titled *Candles in the Wind*, which was republished in 1977.

MARY A. PRYOR (B. 1926) retired in 1992 from Minnesota State University Moorhead where she was Professor of English. She is the author of a collection of poems, *On Occasion*.

GAIL RIXEN (B. 1954) is the author of *Pictures of Three Seasons* and *Chicken Logic*. She farms, teaches writing, and co-edits for Loonfeather Press of Bemidji, Minnesota.

GERALDINE ROSS (1910-1995) was born in Spokane, Washington, but grew up in St. Paul, attending public schools there and furthering her education with continuation and evening courses. For a time she was a librarian at the Minneapolis Public Library. She wrote her first poems when she was nine years old, publishing in the *St. Paul Daily News* and in various journals, including *The Saturday Evening Post* and *The Ladies Home Journal*. She was a great admirer of Keats, and, like Keats, she experimented with the sonnet form. Another of her favorite poets was Sara Teasdale. Ross also wrote children's books, and a number of those books were beautifully illustrated by Kurt Werth, including *Scat, the Witch's Cat*, and *Stop It, Moppit!* In addition to writing her own poems, Ross also reviewed poetry for various publications; her poems in this volume were taken from her collection, *All Kinds of Weather* (1951).

MARY KAY RUMMEL (B. 1941) is the author of *Green Journey, Red Bird; This Body She's Entered; The Long Road Into North*; and a new collection of poetry, *The Illuminations*. Other books include *Teachers' Reading/Teachers' Lives; American Voices: Webs of Diversity*; and *Becoming a Teacher: Connecting Classrooms with Communities*. She is emeritus professor at the University of Minnesota, Duluth, and teaches part-time at California State University, Channel Islands. She currently lives in Fridley, Minnesota.

CAROLANN RUSSELL (B. 1951) is the author of three books of poetry: *The Red Envelope* (1985), *Feast* (1993), and *Silver Dollar* (1995), as well as several limited editions and chapbooks. She has been the recipient of fellowships from the Academy of American Poets, the Ragdale Foundation, the Poetry Society of America, the American Academy in Rome, Italy, and the Minnesota State Arts Board. She was a Jerome Foundation Visiting Poet at the Australia Centre, University of Melbourne. Russell is Professor of Creative Writing and Women's Studies in the Department of English at Bemidji State University.

EDITH RYLANDER (B. 1935) is the author of a collection of poems, *Dancing Back the Cranes* and *Rural Routes: Essays on Living in Rural Minnesota*. In collaboration with her husband John, she wrote *Journeying Earthward*, a memoir of life choices. Her poems have appeared in numerous magazines and anthologies.

ANN TAYLOR SARGENT (B. 1951) is currently working on a parenting memoir, *The Sound of Shoelaces*. She lives in Minneapolis.

ELLIE SCHOENFELD (B. 1958) is the author of *Difficult Valentines, Screaming Red Gladiolas*, and is one of four poets featured in the collection *The Moon Rolls out of Our Mouths*. She lives in Duluth.

IDA SEXTON SEARLS (1854–1938) published poetry in the earliest literary journals in Minnesota, including *Literary Northwest* in the 1890s. She began, in the 1920s, to publish a series of small pamphlets, which contained Native American legends in verse, in the manner of Longfellow. Titles include: *Legend of the Moccasin Flower, Legend of the Water Lily, Nopa, Legend of Shadow Falls, Legend of St. Anthony Falls*, and *Ta-gosh*, this last a tale told to the author by a native of Fond du Lac, where it is set. It is from *Ta-gosh* that the excerpt in this volume is taken. Accounts of the time from the *Minneapolis Journal* describe talks and recitations by Ida Sexton Searls, who would by then have been a woman of about seventy. She was born in Lee Center, Oneida County, New York, and came to Faribault, Minnesota, with her parents at the age of six. She could trace one ancestor, a man named Peter Brown, back to the Mayflower and, though born in 1854, she was in the eighth American generation of her family. She graduated from St. Mary's Hall in 1873, married Silas Wright of Mankato, had two children, and moved to St. Paul in 1883. She was active in many civic organizations, including the Women's Welfare League and the Federation of Women's clubs.

HAZEL BARRINGTON SELBY (1889–1972) was born in Grand Forks, North Dakota, the daughter of pioneers. She also spent time in Montana as a child, and when she married at the age of twenty, she and her new husband sought and won a claim from the U.S. Government for a homestead in the wilderness near Coeur d'Alene, Idaho. They spent three years there, clearing land and going broke in the process. After traveling to many parts of the country, they settled in Minneapolis where they ran a business and raised a family. They had kept the Idaho land, about 350 acres in all and, at the age of sixty, Hazel Barrington Selby and her husband, who was then sixty-five and had suffered a heart attack, returned to the old homestead to reestablish it. This enterprise was the subject of her memoir, *Home to My Mountains*, published five years later in 1962. Her book of poetry was *Stalks of Wind*, from which the work in this volume was taken. It was published in 1941 by B. Humphries, Inc., Boston. She says in her memoir, (italics hers), *"Adventure is the deep and natural element of life on this earth."*

SUN YUNG SHIN (B. 1974) is the author of a collection of poems, *Skirt Full of Black*, co-editor of *Outsiders Within: Racial Crossings and Adoption Politics*, and author of the bilingual (Korean/English) children's book, *Cooper's Lesson*, recipient of a 2004 National Parenting Publication Award for Children's Literature. She lives in Minneapolis, where she is co-editor of WinterRed Press.

GRACE FRENCH SMITH (1879–?) was raised in New York City, graduated from Hunter College and studied at Columbia before becoming a teacher at the Manhattan Teachers Training School. In 1911 she married the

Reverend Thomas W. Smith and moved to Hibbing, where he was pastor of the First Presbyterian Church. She published verse in a number of newspapers and periodicals, including church-oriented publications such as *The Christian Community, Unity,* and *Presbyterian Advance.* Her only book was *Trumpet Call* (1935). The forward, written by Lucia Trent and Ralph Cheyney, praises her for her social activism, as she had "tried to lift burdens from the aching shoulders of fellow-men," offering "the Christian solution to the crushing problems of mankind." These were the years of the Great Depression, "an age ruled over by those who have cash registers in place of hearts." The poems in this volume are taken from *Trumpet Call.*

MADELON SPRENGNETHER (B. 1942) is the author of *The Normal Heart; Rivers, Stories, Houses, Dreams; La Belle et La Bete; Crying at the Movies: A Film Memoir;* and *The Spectral Mother: Freud, Feminism and Psychoanalysis;* and a collection of prose poems, *The Angel of Duluth.* She also co-edited *The House on Via Gombito,* a collection of travel essays by women. She lives in Minneapolis, where she teaches literature and creative writing at the University of Minnesota.

MARION THOMPSON VAN STEENWYK (1907-1976) was born in Superior, Wisconsin. Her family moved to Duluth where she attended Central High School. In 1929, the year she graduated from the University of Minnesota, she married E. A. van Steenwyk, who worked for the company that would become Blue Cross and Blue Shield of Minnesota. He, in fact, designed their signature solid blue Greek cross insignia in 1934. She published her only book of poetry, *Brittle Bright,* in 1931, and the poems we include are taken from that book. She was a member of the League of Minnesota Poets, and she was an associate editor of a travel magazine published in St. Paul called *Globe.* In the 1940s the van Steenwyk family relocated to Pennsylvania, where E. A. van Steenwyk founded and became president of Philadelphia Blue Cross. They bought several hundred of acres, much of it concentrated in a farmstead called "Reddy Run Farm."

SISTER MARIS STELLA (1899-1987). Alice Gustava Smith wrote most often under her religious name, Sister Maris Stella, and published two books of poems: *Here Only a Dove* (1939) and *Frost for Saint Brigid* (1949). Her work appeared in such publications as *Poetry, Commonweal,* and *America.* She was born and raised in Iowa, the daughter of a highly respected physician, F.J.E. Smith, and attended the College of St. Catherine for a year before entering the Sisters of St. Joseph. One of her sisters also joined the religious community of St. Joseph. After her formation, she returned to college and graduated in 1924. She taught for three years and then, in 1927, she enrolled at Oxford University, where she received an M.A. in 1929. Returning to St. Catherine, Sister Maris Stella spent the rest of her career writing and teaching there, and served as chair of the English Department for over twenty years before retiring in 1971. She lived then at Bethany, the retirement home of her religious community, until her death. She is buried in Mendota Heights, Minnesota.

FRANCINE STERLE (B. 1952) is the author of three collections of poems: *The White Bridge* (1999), *Every Bird is One Bird* (2001), and *Nude in Winter* (2006). She earned an M.F.A. in poetry from Warren Wilson College. She lives on the West Two River in northern Minnesota.

JOYCE SUTPHEN (B. 1949) see ABOUT THE EDITORS.

EDITH THOMPSON (1873-1950) was a farm girl, born and raised in Houston, Minnesota, with "calves, pigs, mill ponds, buttercups, mules, chickens, apple trees..." as well as brothers and sisters. She was educated at the local school house, built, she said, with bricks hand made by residents of the district. She studied Latin at the State Teachers College in Mankato, and she took coursework at the University of Minnesota under Dr. Maria Sanford, the first female university professor in America. She said her favorite poet was Wordsworth: "He wrote some of the best and some of the worst poetry in the English language." After a teaching career in several communities, including Red Wing and Minneapolis, she retired to Houston, where she was widely loved. Her book *Romany Riddles* was published in 1929, and a second book called *Lines from a Quarter Section* appeared posthumously in 1962, published by the Houston County Historical Society. We include work from both of these books. She said that she observed gypsies as a girl, and learned some of their tales and customs as they passed by and camped around her father's farm, and the poems in *Romany Riddles* owe their existence to these encounters.

KATRINA VANDENBERG (B. 1971) is the author of *Atlas* (2004), a collection of poems. Vandenberg has been a Fulbright fellow in the Netherlands in 1999–2000, has held an artist residency at the Anderson Center for Interdisciplinary Studies in Redwing, Minnesota, and a Visiting Professorship of Poetry at the University of Arkansas. She lives in St. Paul.

CONNIE WANEK (B. 1952) see ABOUT THE EDITORS.

AMY ROBBINS WARE (1877-1929), daughter of Civil War volunteers (her father a Union soldier, her mother a nurse), traced her ancestors to the Pilgrims on the Mayflower. She was born and lived in Minneapolis and Robbinsdale, though she traveled abroad and was an internationalist, receiving a commendation from President Harding for her work on World Court material, and serving as national president of the Women's Overseas League. She had a strong sense of civic responsibility, and as a Red Cross nurse she served in France during 1918, an experience that she documented in poetry and photographs in her widely admired book, *Echoes of France: Verses from My Journal and Letters* (1920). She was a skilled violinist, taught violin lessons, and played in the community orchestra.

CARY WATERMAN (B. 1942) is the author of *When I Looked Back You Were Gone; The Salamander Migration; First Thaw;* and *Dark Lights the Tiger's Tail.* Her poems have appeared in anthologies such as *A Geography of Poets; Woman Poet: The Midwest; The Logan House Anthology of 21st-Century American Poetry;* and *Poets Against the War.* She is the recipient of Bush Foundation Fellowships, Minnesota State Arts Board Fellowships, and the Loft-McKnight Award of Distinction in Poetry. She teaches at Augsburg College in Minneapolis.

SUSAN STEGER WELSH (B. 1954) is the author of *Rafting on the Water Table.* She lives with her husband and two children in St. Paul.

MARION CRAIG WENTWORTH (1872-1942) was born and raised in Minnesota and attended the University of Minnesota, graduating in 1894. She married in 1900 and had a son; however, she divorced in 1912. She was chiefly known as a playwright. Her early play, *The Flower Shop*, takes up the cause of women's suffrage, and she was always deeply concerned with social issues. In 1915 she wrote her most famous work, a pacifist play called *War Brides.* The play opened on Jan. 25, 1915, at B.F. Keith's Palace Theatre in New York City, and it toured the country for months. In fact it was so popular that an alternate cast took a second production on the road. In 1916 the play was made into a silent film, 48 minutes in length, though by then its pacifist message meant that the film was banned in some communities, and in 1917 the film was re-edited to give it an anti-German bias. The film was very profitable, bringing the studios $300,000. Marion Craig Wentworth wrote several other plays and a beautifully bound book of verse, *Iridescent Days*, from which the poem in this volume was taken. In her later years she traveled a good deal, and her poems reflect this.

GAIL WHITE (1889-1980) was the nom de plume of Gertrude Thomas, born in Detroit, Michigan. She was professor of dietetics at the University of Minnesota, and wrote a number of texts on the subject, including *Foods of Our Forefathers* and *The Dietary of Health and Disease.* She also wrote and published plays for young people, as well as stories and articles and songs, and served as chairman of the drama section of the Faculty Women's Club at the University of Minnesota. Her poetry was collected in *The Phantom Oarsman*, published in 1931, and she continued to publish individual poems in respected journals throughout her life.

JANE WHITLEDGE (B. 1957) works at the Duluth Public Library. Her poems have been published in *33 Minnesota Poets; Yankee; Minnesota Monthly; Wilderness; North Stone Review;* and in numerous other literary magazines.

CARLETON WINSTON (1900-1989) was the pen name of Margaret Carleton, daughter of the prominent Minneapolis attorney, Frank H. Carleton. Margaret Carleton attended schools in Minneapolis and went on to Wells College in Aurora, New York, graduating in 1921. In 1922 she married William O. Winston Jr., a construction engineer, who was also from Minneapolis. For the next seven years, the couple traveled all around the West, and during that time their three children (two girls and a boy) were born. In 1929, Margaret Carleton Winston's young husband was killed in a mining accident, and she returned to Minneapolis with her children. Back in Minneapolis, Carleton Winston concentrated on raising her children and writing poems that could be characterized as intimate and autobiographical. Some of the poems in her single volume, *These Years Passing*, are taken from her early marriage, her life as a widow, and her remarriage to a well-known and controversial Unitarian minister, Dr. John H. Dietrich. Winston married Dietrich in 1933 after his wife had died of cancer in 1931. Dietrich was one of the first Unitarian ministers to preach religious humanism and was a charismatic and popular speaker. During their time in Minneapolis, Carleton Winston was very active in the Minnesota Birth Control League, the Women's International League for Peace, and the League of Minnesota Poets. After many years in Minneapolis, the couple retired to Berkeley, California, where John H. Dietrich died. In 1942, Carleton Winston wrote a warm, intelligent, and interesting biography of her husband's life and work, entitled *This Circle of Earth, The Story of John H. Dietrich*, published in New York by G. P. Putnam's Sons. The book continues to be an excellent resource for anyone interested in the religious history of the time and place. Carleton Winston's poems appeared in many newspapers, poetry magazines, and anthologies, and it is said that she read her own work beautifully.

ABOUT THE ARTIST

ADA AUGUSTA WOLFE (1878-1945) was born in Oakland, California, and moved with her family to Minneapolis when she was eleven years old. As a student at the Minneapolis School of Art, she studied under the school's director Robert Koehler as well as with Gustav Schlegel and Gustave Goetsch. She also studied at the Art Students' League of New York under the guidance of American Impressionist painter William Merritt Chase, one of the most influential teachers of his generation. Among Chase's other pupils were Charles Demuth, Georgia O'Keeffe, and Charles Sheeler. Wolfe returned to Minnesota where she taught art in the Minneapolis schools and frequently exhibited her work in the Twin Cities area. In 1914, *Sails on Lake Minnetonka* won a major prize from the Minnesota State Art Society. Several of her paintings are held in the permanent collection at the Minnesota Historical Society. Wolfe, who hated sentiment in art, said that "If you want to be a painter, then first be a rebel against anything which has a tendency to enslave you. Your attitude of mind is what counts." Her work is included in the beautiful edition *Minnesota Impressionists*, by Rena Neumann Coen, published by the Afton Historical Society Press in 1996.

About the Editors

JOYCE SUTPHEN (B. 1949) is the author of *Straight Out of View*, which won the Barnard New Women's Poets Prize (1995). Her second book of poems, *Coming Back to the Body* (2000), was a finalist for a Minnesota Book Award, and her third book, *Naming the Stars* (2004), won the Minnesota Book Award in Poetry. In 2005, Red Dragonfly Press published a fine-press edition of *Fourteen Sonnets*. Her awards include a Loft-McKnight Award in Poetry, Jerome Fellowships, and a Minnesota State Arts Board Fellowship. She teaches literature and creative writing at Gustavus Adolphus College in St. Peter, Minnesota.

THOM TAMMARO (B. 1951) is the author of two books of poetry, *Holding on for Dear Life* (2004) and *When the Italians Came to My Home Town* (1995), a finalist for a Minnesota Book Award. He is co-editor of *Inheriting the Land: Contemporary Voices from the Midwest* (1993), *Imagining Home: Writing from the Midwest* (1995), and *Visiting Emily: Poems Inspired by the Life and Work of Emily Dickinson* (2000), all recipients of Minnesota Book Awards. He also co-edited *Visiting Walt: Poems Inspired by the Life and Work of Walt Whitman* (2003), a finalist for a Minnesota Book Award, and *Visiting Frost: Poems Inspired by the Life and Work of Robert Frost* (2005). He lives in Moorhead, Minnesota, where he is Professor of English at Minnesota State University.

CONNIE WANEK (B. 1952) is the author of two books of poetry: *Bonfire* (1997) and *Hartley Field* (2002). Her poems have appeared in *Poetry*, *The Atlantic Monthly*, *The Virginia Quarterly*, and many other journals, and she has received several prizes including the Jane Kenyon Poetry Prize. She has received fellowship support from the Jerome Foundation and the Arrowhead Regional Arts Council. Ted Kooser named her a Witter Bynner Fellow of the Library of Congress for 2006, and has included her work in his *American Life in Poetry* newspaper column. She has two grown children and works at the Duluth Public Library.

Permissions

We are grateful to the authors, editors, publishers and literary executors who have provided permission to reprint poems. All reasonable attempts were made to locate the original copyright holders. Any errors or oversights brought to our attention will be corrected and acknowledged in subsequent printings.

Patricia Barone, "Last Night on a Northern Lake." Copyright © 2006 by Patricia Barone. Reprinted by permission of the author.

Sandy Beach, "Slow Brown Fox." Copyright © 2005 by Sandy Beach. Reprinted by permission of the author.

Candace Black, "Vigil," originally appeared in *The Pharos*. Reprinted in *The Volunteer* (New Rivers Press, 2003). Copyright © 2003 by Candace Black. Reprinted by permission of New Rivers Press and the author.

Lily Lawrence Bow, "Blossom Time." Reprinted from *Wind in the Palm Trees Singing* (Homestead, Florida: Cycle Press, 1937).

Jill Breckenridge, "Jacob" and "Will Sommer, Confederate Soldier." From *Civil Blood* (Milkweed Editions, 1986). Copyright © 1986 by Jill Breckenridge. Reprinted by permission of the author.

Betty Bridgman, "The Tire Swing" and "Letter of Introduction." From *This Is Minnesota* (St. Paul: North Central Publishing Co., 1958). Copyright © 1958 by Betty Bridgman. Reprinted by permission of George H. Bridgman, Literary Executor, The Estate of Betty Bridgman.

Ruth F. Brin, "September." From *Harvest: Collected Poems & Prayers* (Holy Cow! Press; 2nd Revised edition, 1999). Copyright © 1999 by Ruth F. Brin. Reprinted by permission of the publisher.

Carol Ryrie Brink, "The Nun" and "Bones of the Martyrs" were originally published in *The Gypsy*, 1926 and 1934, respectively; "The Nun" reprinted in *Minnesota Verse* edited by Maude Schilplin (St. Cloud, Minnsota: Times Publishing Company, 1938); "New York Hotel" was originally published in *Shreds and Patches* (Minneapolis. Privately printed in 1978). Reprinted by permission of The Estate of Carol Ryrie Brink.

Lucille Broderson, "Letter Never Sent." From *33 Minnesota Poets* (2000). Copyright © 2000 by Lucille Broderson. Reprinted by permission of the author.

Alison Brown, "On St. Louis Bay." Reprinted from *Lake Superior Magic* (Duluth, MN: Mattocks McDonald Co., 1927).

Betsy Brown, "Hallways of a Diamond: January 2004." Copyright © 2006 by Betsy Brown. Reprinted by permission of the author.

Nellie Manley Buck, "Bobbed Hair." Reprinted from *By Winding Trails* (Boston: Christopher Publishing House, 1928).

Cullen Bailey Burns, "I Have Made A Paper Boat." From *Paper Boat* (New Rivers Press, 2003). Copyright © 2003 by Cullen Bailey Burns. Reprinted by permission of New Rivers Press and the author.

Marisha Chamberlain, "Winter Washday," originally appeared in *Dacotah Territory*. Copyright © 1983 by Marisha Chamberlin. Reprinted by permission of the author.

Sharon Chmielarz, "Another Love Letter," originally appeared in *Water~Stone Review*, Vol 7, Fall 2004. Copyright © 2004 by Sharon Chmielarz. Reprinted by permission of the author.

Marianne Clarke, "Connecting Stars." Reprinted from *Miss America* (New York: Leach Naylor Green-Leach, Publisher, 1929). Copyright © 1929 by Marianne Clarke.

Clara A. Clausen, "The Weaver," "The Trees" and "Silver Land." Reprinted from *Silver Land* (Kenyon, Minnesota: *The Kenyon Leader*, 1934). Copyright © 1934 by Clara A. Clausen.

Carol Connolly, "Shallows." From *Payments Due* (Midwest Villages & Voices, 1995). Copyright © 1995 by Carol Connolly. Reprinted by permission of the author.

Grace Noll Crowell, "The Girl That I Used To Be" and "White Fire." Reprinted from *White Fire* (Fort Worth, TX, 1925, 1928. Reprinted by Harper, 1934). Copyright © 1925 by Grace Noll Crowell.

Florence Chard Dacey, "Threshold." Copyright © 2006 by Florence Chard Dacey. Reprinted by permission of the author.